KAY'S
ANATOMY

T0018580

Adam Kay is a former doctor who has sold over three million books. Hang on—maybe it was just one person who bought three million copies. Thanks if that was you!

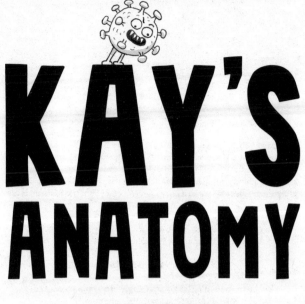

KAY'S
ANATOMY

A COMPLETE
(AND COMPLETELY DISGUSTING)
GUIDE TO THE
HUMAN BODY

 ADAM KAY

ILLUSTRATED BY **HENRY PAKER**

A YEARLING BOOK

Text copyright © 2020 by Adam Kay
Cover art copyright © 2022 by Henry Paker
Interior illustrations copyright © 2020 by Henry Paker

All rights reserved. Published in the United States by Yearling, an imprint of
Random House Children's Books, a division of Penguin Random House LLC, New York.
Originally published in hardcover by Penguin Books, an imprint of Penguin Random House UK,
London, in 2020. Subsequently published in hardcover in the United States by Delacorte Press,
an imprint of Random House Children's Books, a division of Penguin Random House LLC,
New York, in 2022.

Yearling and the jumping horse design are registered trademarks
of Penguin Random House LLC.

Visit us on the Web! rhcbooks.com

Educators and librarians, for a variety of teaching tools,
visit us at RHTeachersLibrarians.com

The Library of Congress has cataloged the hardcover edition of this work as follows:
Names: Kay, Adam, author. | Paker, Henry, illustrator.
Title: Kay's anatomy : A complete (and completely disgusting) guide to the human
body / Adam Kay ; illustrated by Henry Paker.
Description: New York : Delacorte Press, 2022. | Includes index. | Audience: Ages 8–12 |
Summary: "A complete (and completely gross) guide to the human body for
middle grade readers"— Provided by publisher.
Identifiers: LCCN 2021015632 (print) | LCCN 2021015633 (ebook) |
ISBN 978-0-593-48340-4 (hardcover) | ISBN 978-0-593-48343-5 (library binding) |
ISBN 978-0-593-48341-1 (ebook)
Subjects: LCSH: Human body—Juvenile literature. | Human body—Humor—Juvenile literature.
Classification: LCC QP37 .K355 2022 (print) | LCC QP37 (ebook) | DDC 612—dc23

ISBN 978-0-593-48342-8 (paperback)

Printed in the United States of America
10 9 8 7 6 5 4 3 2 1
First Yearling Edition 2023

To my science teacher Mr. Andrews,
who gave me a detention in 1991 for
saying that he smelled.

Well, he did smell, and I bet he still smells,
and now it's official because it's in a book.

CONTENTS

INTRODUCTION

DO YOU EVER THINK about your body? Like really, *really* think about it? I mean, sure, you can't help it when you've stubbed your toe or you've got an earache or you've caught a stomach bug and feel like you're going to literally poop out your guts and your lungs and your brain, but . . . do you know what's actually going on in there?

Have you ever thought that your body is just a strange lump of meat, held up by a big pile of bones, wrapped in a bag of skin, and all controlled by a crazy supercomputer in your head? Oh, you haven't? Sorry if I've freaked you out. But what I'm saying is your body is *weird*. I don't mean to be rude. Everybody's body is weird—yours, mine, your parents', your math teacher's. Especially your math teacher's.

YOUR MATH TEACHER'S BODY

ACTUALLY, WE DECIDED THIS WAS TOO WEIRD TO SHOW YOU.

You never get to see what's inside your body, do you? Not unless you've cut yourself and a bit of red stuff has oozed out, or maybe if you've been for an X-ray. But you can't just look inside yourself any time you like. Even if you go to a mirror and open your mouth very wide—I'm talking hippo-yawn wide here—and try to look down your throat, all you'll see is a tongue, some teeth, and a set of tonsils, and then . . . it goes dark. What's it hiding?

I know they teach you some stuff about the body at school. I also know there's no quicker way to make something boring than forcing you to sit on an uncomfortable plastic chair and learn about it from a whiteboard. But just because your teacher might be boring, that doesn't mean the thing they're telling you about is. The human body is a scientific marvel—an incredible machine that's been perfected over the last seven million years, give or take a few days. It's more advanced than a space station and smarter than the speediest super-computer. I'm not kidding—your brain can process 400 billion things a second. And 400 billion is massive. If you wanted to count to 400 billion, it would take you over twelve thousand years. (Don't try, or you'll miss dinner.)

LOOK, I GET IT. When you're given a new toy, the last thing you want to do is read the instruction manual— you just want to start playing with it. But you've had your body for years and years now, and I bet you don't know half the things it can do. It's finally time to open the instructions.

I'm going to take you through the body, organ by organ. When I say "take you through" it, don't panic, I'm not going to dress you up in rain boots and a waterproof jacket, put you into a shrinking machine, and make you wade through miles of intestines. Firstly, I'm not totally sure that shrinking machines exist. Secondly, we'd get absolutely covered in poop. Not to say there won't be poop in the book—how could there not be? We all do it. Even your math teacher. Sorry, I didn't mean to make you think of your math teacher pooping. By the way, did you know that about a quarter of your poop is *alive*?! Don't worry, you're not about to get attacked by zombie turds—it's just bacteria. Well, I say *just*—there's trillions of them in there. In fact, there are more bacteria in every poop you do than there are pages on the entire internet.

Let's find out all of your body's weird and wonderful secrets. Like the brain, for instance, which feels no pain. You could take a big stick and mush it around your brain and it wouldn't hurt at all. (Please don't take a big stick and mush it around your brain.)

WELL, THIS WAS POINTLESS.

Then there's your heart, which it turns out is neither bright pink nor heart-shaped, so someone should urgently tell whoever makes Valentine's Day cards. And it pumps enough blood around your body each day to fill ninety (pretty repulsive) bathtubs. And how about your lungs, which puff out enough air every day to blow up a thousand balloons? Who needs a thousand balloons for their birthday? Save a bit of breath to sing "Happy Birthday," for goodness' sake.

X-RAY

Like a sightseeing tour, we'll take in all the best bits, such as the skin, which is the largest organ in the human body and the one you'd look the weirdest without. But did you know your skin isn't actually your outermost part? Wherever you go, you're always surrounded by an invisible cloud. "A cloud! How cute!" Nope. It's a cloud of thousands of tiny bits of skin that flake off you, along with cells that come out of your various giblets every time you speak, yawn, burp, or fart. And if you think that's disgusting, wait until I tell you about the weird creatures who live in your eyelashes. Or worse still, what they eat for dinner.

How do you know I'm not making this all up? Well, I worked as a doctor for years and years. These days I write books, but hopefully I haven't forgotten *too* much about how the body works. It would be a real shame if I was teaching you a load of absolute nonsense, but I guess you won't know until you fail your exams. So you're probably just going to have to trust me. . . .

In this book I'm going to answer every question you could possibly have about the human body, including the things your teachers and parents quickly change the subject about when you ask them. (Probably because they don't know the answers. Idiots.)

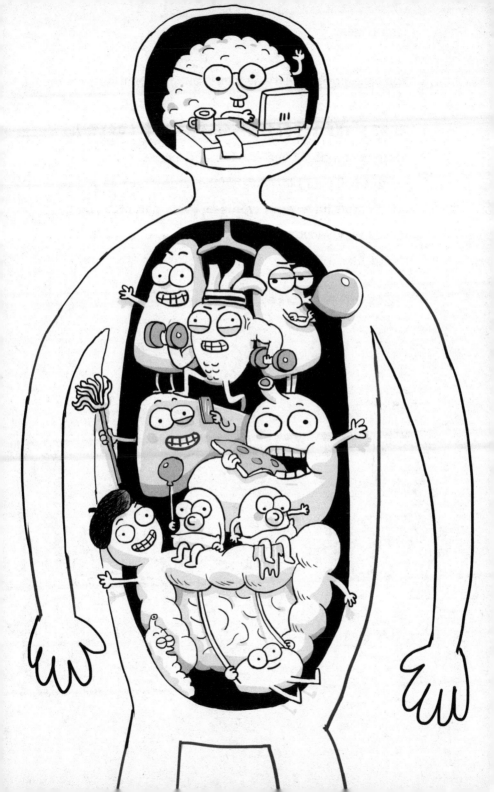

You can expect questions like:

WHAT'S THE LARGEST MUSCLE IN THE BODY? No,

gluteus maximus isn't a Roman emperor, it's what doctors call your butt, and it's the largest muscle you've got. Doctors have fancy words for every part of the body, by the way. Mostly so we don't have to constantly say things like "butt."

ARE BOOGERS SAFE TO EAT? Look, if your nose is going to all that effort of creating a snack, the least we can do is look at its nutritional value, right? (Yes, they're safe. Chew away!)

WAITER, THERE'S A FLY ON MY BOOGER!

HOW MUCH OF YOUR LIFE WILL YOU SPEND ON THE TOILET? About a year—so bring a good book. (I recommend this one.)

And there are hundreds more where those came from.

I'll also explain how your body can sometimes get wonky. Just like a tablet can crash when you update an app, your body is another complicated bit of equipment that malfunctions from time to time. I'll tell you exactly what it means to have conditions that you or your friends might already live with, like epilepsy or diabetes or asthma, as well as the everyday stuff that never seems to get you a day off school. I'm talking colds and bruises, and the dreaded face art that is an attack of pimples. Basically, anything that makes you ask, "Why on earth is this happening to *me*?"

Speaking of which, we'll take a look at some of the changes your body goes through as it prepares you for adulthood. It's not all wearing ties, drinking coffee, and shouting at people, you know. Puberty is a bit like transforming into a totally new person who looks like a squeezed and stretched-out version of you, so I'll explain about all that, and the feelings you might be dealing with too.

We'll take a look at the things your body would probably rather you didn't do, such as smoking, using drugs and alcohol, eating unhealthy food, and not getting enough sleep or exercise. No judging, no taking your phone off you for a week; just telling you what's what. Your body belongs to you, after all—you can do what you like with it. (Though maybe don't go snowboarding in your underwear.)

So if you're ready to learn things that you can't possibly unknow and to be furnished with facts that, while incredible, you probably shouldn't repeat at the dinner table, then this is the book for you. Take a seat, let your creepy cloud of dead skin and poo-dust settle around you, and welcome to . . .

KAY'S ANATOMY

AN ORGAN is a large musical instrument with a couple of keyboards, loads of different pedals, and some massive pipes. (An organ can also mean a part of your body that does a specific thing.)

HEART — PUMPS BLOOD

LUNGS — PUMP AIR

BRAIN — PUMPS NOTHING
(BUT IT'S STILL FAIRLY USEFUL)

STOMACH — WHERE
FOOD GOES

INTESTINES — MAKE POOP

KIDNEYS — MAKE PEE

LIVER — CLEANS UP YOUR BLOOD

CELLS — THE LITTLE LUMPS OF LEGO THAT EVERY ORGAN IS MADE OF

BACTERIA & VIRUSES — ANNOYING AND INFECTING

PIPPIN — MY DOG. NOT REALLY PART OF THE BODY, BUT CUTE, ISN'T SHE?

CHAPTER 1

SKIN

THANK GOODNESS FOR SKIN. Can you imagine the absolute mess you'd make when you walked around if you didn't have any? Flesh dangling off your bones. Various innards trailing behind you. Actually, let's stop imagining that—I'm feeling a bit sick now. It might just look like a very tight onesie, but your skin is actually an extremely sophisticated organ. You never think of your skin really weighing anything, do you? But in the unfortunate event that it was separated from the rest of your body and chucked on the bathroom scale, an adult's skin would come to somewhere between 9 and 18 pounds (depending on how tall they are)—that's heavier than some bowling balls.

Like everything else in your body, your skin is made up of cells—35 billion of them, to be precise. 35 billion is quite a lot, by the way. If you stood 35 billion hamsters in a line, they would stretch all the way around the sun. (Please don't do this, because their feet would get very sore.)

Your skin totally replaces itself every few weeks. It's a bit like getting a brand-new outfit once a month—except you don't get to choose its design and you can't add sequins to it. The amount of skin you shed in a lifetime would fill a (horrendous) wheelbarrow.

How thick your skin is depends on where it is on your body. (I mean the depth of your skin, by the way, not how easily offended you are.) It's thickest on the bottom of your feet; otherwise they'd be covered with holes like a worn-out pair of socks, and it's thinnest on your eyelids, because otherwise you'd have to pry them open with your fingers every morning and there would be a loud clunking noise every time you blinked.

Skin cells replicate themselves faster than any other cells in your body—you make millions and millions of new cells every single day. So next time some annoying adult accuses you of being lazy because you've been playing computer games for five hours, you can simply explain that you were actually making huge numbers of skin cells.

And what happens with your old skin? You obviously don't just get wider and wider until you can't fit through the front door. Well (and I hope you're sitting down while I break this to you), you shed. Not in one go like a snake, but constantly. See that dust all over your bedroom because you refuse to clean it until your allowance gets increased? It might be time to grab the vacuum, because that dust is mostly flakes of . . . you. Whoops—there go another couple of thousand skin cells. And a few thousand more. If you could see them coming off, it would look like you were snowing some quite disgusting snow.

Let's take a quick break from this revoltingness so I can tell you about my dog, Pippin. She's one year old, she's an Airedale terrier, and her hobbies include taking walks, drinking from puddles, and getting sick on the sofa.

Do you have any pets? How many? Nope—wrong answer. You've actually got millions and millions and millions of them . . . all over your skin. Sorry, we're back to the revoltingness already.

Viruses and bacteria and various types of fungus and tiny insects rub shoulders on every inch of you. (Well, they don't actually have shoulders, but you get the idea.) It's nothing to worry about—they're just a bunch of laid-back dudes getting on with their day and keeping your skin safe and healthy. All of this means that you're surrounded every second of the day by a cloud of germs and dead skin. Oh, and particles of fart too, which should probably be called farticles. So next time you hug a friend or a parent, you now know that you're covering them in your farty skin-cloud. Mwahaha! The downside is that they're also covering *you* in *their* farty skin-cloud. Ugh.

LAYERS OF THE SKIN

Unlike your robot butler, who's only covered in a single sheet of metal, your skin is made up of various layers, like a horrible dry lasagne. (Oh, you don't have a robot butler? Shame. Mine's making me a chocolate milkshake right now.)

ONE MILKSHAKE COMING UP.

EPIDERMIS — This is the top layer: the bit that you can see and touch. You know how when you put pasta in water, it soaks it up and gets much bigger and floppier? Well, why doesn't that happen to you when you go swimming? It's all thanks to your epidermis keeping you waterproof. Your skin color also depends on your epidermis, because it contains melanin. (Not to be confused with a fruit salad, which has melon in it.) The

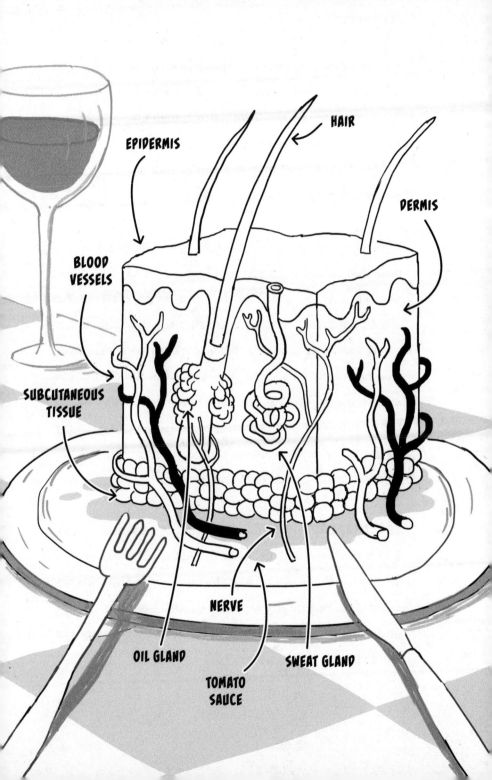

more melanin you have, the darker your skin color; the less melanin you have, the lighter your skin color. Also in the epidermis are freckles— harmless little patches of melanin that are unique to you, and that you can use for a game of connect-the-dots if you get bored.

DERMIS — Head down a level to your dermis and there's *a lot* going on. There are a load of blood vessels and nerves, as well as your sweat and oil glands, which keep your skin from getting too dry. This is the strongest layer, and it's what prevents your skin from ripping like plastic wrap. The dermis is the part of the skin that contains your fingerprints, and it's also where tattoo ink goes. I'm thinking of getting a tattoo of my eyes on my eyelids so no one will know when I fall asleep during boring conversations.

SUBCUTANEOUS TISSUE — This is the basement layer, and it's where your fat lives. However thin we are, we all have a layer of fat, and it's very good that we do, because it keeps us warm and protects us from bumps and falls. It's like a massive shin pad that covers our whole body.

FUNCTIONS OF THE SKIN

Your skin is more than a walking tote bag that makes sure your insides don't end up as your outsides. It has lots of other important functions, such as controlling your temperature, enabling your sense of touch, and turning bright green every Wednesday. (One of these might not be 100 percent true.)

TEMPERATURE CONTROL

Chuck that electric fan in the trash and rip the radiators off the wall—your skin has all sorts of schemes and wheezes to keep you at a toasty 98.6 degrees— which, funnily enough, is known as body temperature. If it's hot outside or if you've been doing something energetic like carrying a horse (you weirdo), then your body turns on its sprinkler system to cool you right down again. Your brain tells the sweat glands deep in your dermis to get busy, and they send sweat up little tubes shaped like strings of spaghetti. Sweat comes out of tiny little holes called pores. They're too small to see, so you'll have to

Your skin is also known as the **cutaneous system**. Because it's really cute. Actually, it's probably Latin or something— usually is.

trust me on this, but you've got millions and millions of holes all over your skin. You're basically a massive sieve.

On hot days or if you've been running (for example, if your robot butler has malfunctioned and is chasing you around your bedroom), then you can lose loads of fluid through sweat, so it's very important that you drink a lot to replace everything that has escaped out of your skin. If you don't, then you risk getting dehydrated—this can make you feel tired, give you a headache, or even make you faint. So grab a glass of water, or, if you're Pippin, drink from a disgusting puddle.

How about when it's a cold day? Well, your skin has another trick up its furry little sleeve. Tiny hairs on your arms and legs stand on end,

Your lips are one of only a few parts of the body that don't have any sweat glands— that's why they can get dry and chapped when it's hot. No one really knows why they don't sweat— maybe it's because deodorant doesn't taste very nice.

trapping a thin layer of air right next to your skin and keeping you warm like an invisible sweater. You may know this feeling as "goose bumps." Or, if you're a goose, you may know it as "bumps." Ever noticed how your fingers and toes get cold the fastest when it's freezing outside? That's your brain deciding that it's less important for your blood to go to your skin and more important that it go to . . . itself. A bit selfish, if you ask me.

Your sweat doesn't actually have any smell at all. At least, it doesn't when it's fresh out of your sweat glands. It only gets its traditional whiff when the bacteria that live on your skin have it as a refreshing drink.

PROTECTION

Skin is your first line of defense against the outside world. It stops you from getting infections, it means you don't get damaged by heat, and it prevents injuries. And do you ever stop to thank your skin for doing all this? Do you? Say thanks to your skin for protecting you. Go on, do it now, I'll wait.

Done? Okay, let's go on.

TOUCH

Your sense of touch is really important. It sends messages to your brain to tell it if you're safe, or whether there's something dangerous you need to know about. Are you wet, or hot, or cold, or in pain? That's up to your skin to find out—and to do this it uses millions and millions of receptors. It has different types of these receptors to detect things like gentle touch, sharp touch, deep pressure, vibrations, temperature, and pain. For anything you need to feel, your skin's got you covered. (Literally.) Some areas, such as your fingertips, have many more receptors than others—that's why it feels like the end of the world if you get a paper cut. I got about fifty paper cuts writing this book, so I hope you're feeling very sorry for me right now. If the nerve endings in your skin feel pain, they send a message straight to your brain.

Dear Brain,

Just to say that it feels like our right foot is standing on a piece of Lego. You might want to lift this leg up urgently, and tell the mouth to scream quite loudly. Whenever is convenient, although I do recommend doing it immediately.

Lots of love, Skin xx

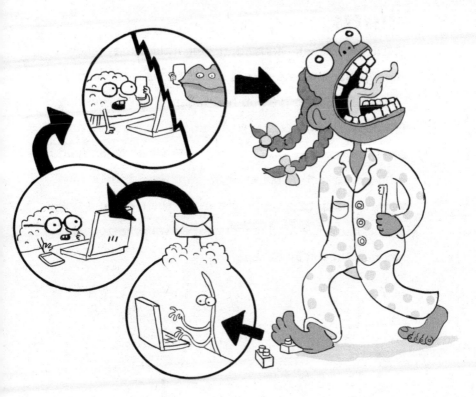

LUMPS AND BUMPS

Unless you spend your life in a house built out of cotton
balls, wearing a hat made from feathers and a
marshmallow tracksuit, you'll find yourself getting cuts
and scrapes and blisters and bruises. Here's what your
skin is really up to when it goes multicolored.

BLISTERS

You know blisters—those annoying little watery pillows that appear if a new pair of school shoes is rubbing on your skin, or if you've climbed Mount Everest wearing flip-flops. This friction on your skin makes the epidermis separate from the dermis underneath, and some fluid (plasma, in fact) leaks into the gap. Now, I realize it's very tempting to pop the blister and see how far it will squirt, like some kind of foot-shaped water pistol, but I recommend you avoid that.

Firstly, the fluid in the blister is there to do a job and will help you heal quicker. Secondly, remember how your skin has to keep you safe from germs? Well, that's rather difficult if you're bursting it like Bubble Wrap all the time. You even risk causing a serious infection. This happened to my friend Nick—he popped a blister on his foot and it got so disgusting and pus-filled that he had to go to the hospital. (When he texted me a photo of it, I was almost sick.) Leave your blister alone and it'll disappear on its own in a few days.

BRUISES

When a wall isn't looking where it's going and thoughtlessly bumps into you, you might end up with a bruise. This means you've damaged the blood vessels in your skin and a bit of blood has leaked out. Because you haven't cut your skin, the blood doesn't have anywhere to go, so it spreads out underneath. One bruise, coming right up.

Bruises change color over the week or two when they're loitering under your skin, a bit like a disgusting set of traffic lights. They start off red, which is fair enough, because that's the color of blood. But after a day or so, the bruise starts redecorating. First, it goes sort of bluey-blacky-purple, because the oxygen in your blood has been used up. Then the blood starts to dissolve, and your bruise will go green, and then finally, after a week or so, it will fade to its final color: yellow. Blood vessels in the skin get weaker with age, so older people are more likely to get a bruise if they clonk themselves. In other words, maybe you should tell Grandma to give up ski jumping.

ECZEMA

We all get dry skin once in a while, but there's a very common condition called eczema where you have dry and itchy skin a lot of the time. It often affects the insides of the elbows or the knees but can occur anywhere. It's not contagious (which means you can't catch it from other people), it can be treated with creams and ointments, and it's really difficult to spell.

BURNS

It's extremely important to be careful around anything that might be hot—for example, saucepans, irons, kettles, hair straighteners, hot drinks, and volcanoes. First-degree burns are the most common sort of burn, and they make your skin go red. This means the burn has only affected the epidermis and will almost always heal very well. Second-degree burns are deeper and go through into the dermis—this can cause blisters on the skin, and only occasionally causes scarring. Third-degree burns are the most serious, where the burn goes right down into the subcutaneous tissue. A third-degree burn will always need hospital attention, sometimes even surgery, and it often causes scarring. If you burn yourself, you need to call an adult for help and then run the bit you've burned under cold water for about twenty minutes. (I know, I know. That's a long time and you're very busy—but it really is important.) You might need to go to the hospital to get checked out, or you might need to do an impression of a cheese sandwich and have the burn covered in plastic wrap—this makes it less likely that you'll get an infection.

SCARS

How many scars have you managed to achieve over your lifetime so far? Whether it was the result of an operation or a disagreement between your face and the pavement, chances are you've got a scar or two somewhere on that big bag of skin you wear. Even though your skin is very good at mending itself, if the damage goes right to the dermis then it sometimes leaves a mark. This is because of a substance called collagen, which is basically a type of cement your body uses to repair injuries deep down in the skin. Collagen is very effective at gluing you back together, but it can leave a white mark. Scars fade with time but may never totally disappear. I've still got a scar on my forehead from accidentally running into a server holding a metal tray when I was eight. (No need to worry, she didn't spill any food.) Scars can be a good conversation starter with new friends, especially if you make up the reasons you got them, such as a swordfight with a kitten or rescuing a bank robber from a burning building. Hang on, I meant a swordfight with a bank robber or rescuing a kitten from a burning building. You should never be ashamed of your scars, but that said, please try not to pick up any new ones. . . .

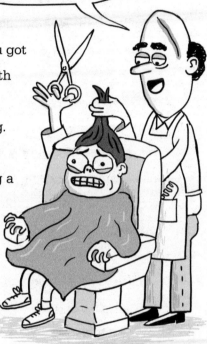

HOW DID I GET THIS SCAR? WELL, IT ALL HAPPENED THE LAST TIME I CUT SOMEONE'S HAIR . . .

SUN DAMAGE

The sun is important for our bodies—it helps us produce vitamin D, which we need to keep our bones healthy. But there can always be too much of a good thing (apart from TV), and the sun is also one of our skin's biggest enemies. Sunlight contains harmful ultraviolet rays, which damage the dermis. It wrinkles your skin and causes permanent changes that could one day become life-threatening skin cancer. That's why it's so important to always cover up on hot days and plaster on plenty of sunscreen; otherwise you'll end up looking like a wrinkled old raisin with a face drawn on it, and no one wants that.

PIMPLES

You might be lucky enough not to have experienced pimples yet. Or maybe you'll never get any. But, for many of us, pimples are a fact of life. For most people, their first experience with pimples comes around the time of puberty.

Why is there a huge pimple on the end of your nose? Has an evil wizard put a curse on you? Probably not (but no promises). Pimples happen when the oil glands in your skin get clogged. Instead of doing their job, which is to moisturize the skin, sometimes they go rogue and fill up with excess oil

WHAT A BEAUTIFUL VIEW!

and dead skin cells. This turns them into things called whiteheads and blackheads. They can also get inflamed or infected and turn into red pimples.

Almost everyone gets pimples, and it's totally normal (even if it feels monumentally unfair). Having pimples can make you feel pretty miserable, especially if people with awful personalities make fun of you. But remember, pimples don't last forever—they'll be gone and forgotten before long—but those people will have awful personalities for the rest of their lives.

Acne isn't caused by eating junk food (although that's not an excuse to eat forty-nine pepperoni pizzas tonight), and it doesn't happen because you're not washing enough either. Pimples are caused by what's going on underneath your skin—in fact, washing your face too much can actually make them worse. And acne isn't contagious— you can't pass it on or catch it from other people.

If you get acne, use very mild soap to clean your face, and avoid wearing makeup, if that's something you do. Keep your hair nice and clean, and try to keep it off your face. If you're worried that your acne is severe, or if it's getting you down, or if you get pimples on your chest and back, then go to see a doctor about it, because some people's acne can improve with medicine. (Don't be nervous or embarrassed about seeing a doctor—they see *hundreds* of people with the same issue. Besides, they'd be out of a job if all their patients stayed at home all day.) Most importantly, remember that your acne will disappear one day, just as quickly as it turned up in the first place.

IMPETIGO

If there are a couple of words you probably don't want describing your face, let me suggest "crusty" and "blistered." Impetigo is a skin infection that causes crusty yellow blisters, commonly around the nose and mouth. It's very contagious, so not something to be prodding with your fingers. It normally clears up nicely with antibiotics.

BIRTHMARKS

Life would be extremely boring if we all looked the same, like an army of identical androids. Also, it would be very difficult to find your parents in the supermarket. Our skins all have their own color or shade, and they each have their own little quirks and differences too. Your skin is a customized map, just for you. Some of these things your body adds over time, like scars from chicken pox, injuries, and operations, but some you are just born with. We call these birthmarks (for reasons you can probably guess) and usually they're totally harmless—just part of who you are. Some are red or purple (known as port wine stains) and some are light brown (known as café-au-lait spots, which means "milky coffee" in French—whoever was naming birthmarks must have been really thirsty). Most of us also have moles, which are small black or brown marks on the skin. Most moles are nothing to worry about, but sometimes a mole can in fact be skin cancer. That's why it's important to tell someone if a mole has done one of the following things: changed shape, changed color, gotten bigger, started bleeding, started itching, or dug up your garden. (Sorry, wrong type of mole.)

KAY'S KWESTIONS

WHY CAN'T WE TICKLE OURSELVES?

Because you know it's coming. Your brain is programmed to react if it notices an unexpected crawling sensation on your skin (in case it's a

Sorry for the bad spelling there. Pippin was sick on my laptop and now the letter   doesn't always work. Sorry, I meant the letter   .
Whoops—the letter Q. See what I mean?

massive man-eating tarantula), and that's why tickling feels so weird/great/awful—delete as appropriate. But if you try to tickle *yourself,* your brain knows it's you who's doing it, so doesn't react the same way.

WHY DOES YOUR SKIN GET WRINKLY IN THE BATHTUB?

If you've ever spent ages in the bathtub (I hope you remembered to put bubble bath in), then you might have noticed your hands and feet start to go wrinkly. Scientists think these wrinkles happen to help you grip things better when your hands are wet—a bit like how car tires have grooves in them so they don't slide around on the road. Unfortunately, this only helps you grip a tiny bit better—no climbing up the outside of your house like Spider-Man, I'm afraid.

WHY DOES SEEING SOMEONE ITCHING MAKE YOU FEEL ITCHY TOO?

You probably get itchy if you see someone else scratching themselves. Your brain does this to warn you that you might be covered in the same little bugs as the person you can see scratching. Some people get itchy just seeing the word itch. *Itch!* (Did that work? Don't scratch too hard—mustn't damage that lovely skin of yours.)

TRUE OR POO?

SQUEEZING A PIMPLE MAKES IT WORSE.

TRUE Sorry about this, but even if you're dying to do it, squeezing your pimple is pretty much the worst thing you can do. It opens you up to infection—the billions of bacteria who live on your skin would love a free holiday underneath. If you squeeze it, you might even turn your pimple into a scar. Consider yourself warned!

IDENTICAL TWINS HAVE THE SAME FINGERPRINTS.

POO I guess they're not totally identical after all. Your fingerprints are unique. Not one person out of the billions of people on Earth has the same fingerprints as you. This is because your fingerprints are formed by tons of different things that happen before you're born, such as the position you were lying in, inside the uterus.

DOCTORS USE MAGGOTS TO HELP WOUNDS HEAL.

TRUE Disgusting, but true. If a patient has a lot of dead or infected tissue on their skin that doctors need to remove, they can use maggots to get the job done. When maggots are put onto a wound, they vomit special chemicals that break up the flesh, and then they eat it all back up. That's right, they puke on you, and then not only do they eat you but they also eat their own vomit. In summary, maggots are very handy for doctors but terrible dinner companions.

EATING TOO MANY CARROTS CAN MAKE YOUR SKIN TURN ORANGE.

TRUE If you ate loads and loads and loads of carrots for ages and ages and ages, then you would end up with high levels of a substance called beta-carotene in your bloodstream, which would cause parts of your skin (such as the palms of your hands) to turn orange. The treatment is very simple—stop eating so many carrots!

CAN YOU SOMETIMES HEAR a faint little drumbeat? Maybe when you've been running around, or when you're sitting totally still in a room with the TV off. Do you know what that sound is? That's right—it's Nigel from next door practicing his timpani. I wish he'd stop, it's impossible to get any sleep around here.

My mistake. It's actually your heart—sitting inside your rib cage, not-so-quietly getting on with things. No big deal.

Except, of course, it's a very big deal. Just like a car can't start without an engine, or you can't do your homework without a big bag of chips (actually, make that two bags, to be on the safe side), nothing happens in your body without your heart pumping away. Not bad for an organ that's only the size of your fist.

The heart is the fifth-biggest organ in your body. In at number four are the lungs—but they should probably be disqualified for cheating because there are two of them. Number three is that old smart aleck, the brain. At number two is your big lump of liver, and at number one is that stretchy bag of weirdness: your skin.

HOW IT WORKS

The heart is a muscle, a bit like the muscles you have in your arms and your legs. The thing that's special about your heart, though, is that you *choose* when to waggle your limbs, but the heart doesn't need your permission to beat. It's just as well, because your heart can't take a second's rest, even when you're asleep, because if it did . . . well, that would be pretty serious. And no other bit of your body can step in and cover its work—there's no such thing as a substitute teacher for the heart.

The heart sits in the middle of your chest, slightly over to the left, nestled between your lungs. They definitely need to fire whoever came up with the little ♥ symbol.

Your actual heart is more of a splodge shape, and it's certainly not a cute shade of pink. It's a much darker red. Blood red, you might say. Well, you could definitely say that, because every single drop of blood in your body passes through your heart. That's what it's doing with all its pumping—sending blood around your body. You might be wondering why it does this. (To be honest, if you're not wondering, then you can probably skip a couple of pages.) It's not just a weird hobby it's taken up because it doesn't have an Xbox: it's all about oxygen. Every single millimeter of your body from your tongue to your thumb to your butt needs oxygen to live, and your heart makes sure the oxygen gets there. (Sorry, I've lied to you slightly. There's one part of your body that doesn't get any blood at all—it's called the cornea, and it's the layer on the outside of your eye. It still needs oxygen, but it gets it directly from the air. There's always someone who wants to be different, huh?)

The heart is divided into left and right sides, and each side is divided into two chambers—so how many chambers is that in total? That's right: sixteen thousand, two hundred and thirty-eight. Hold on—I pressed the wrong button on my calculator. It's actually four. The heart is made up of four chambers, and each one is like the room of a house. A quite disgusting house, because it's totally full of blood. Also, it's way too small to live in, unless you're a fly. And you probably don't want a fly living in your heart. That would cause a very serious condition called . . . umm . . . fly-in-your-heart-itis.

Blood enters your heart on the left side into the top chamber (called an atrium), and the blood is full of lovely oxygen, because it's just come from the lungs. It then flows down to the bottom chamber (or ventricle), where it gets an almighty *SQUEEZE* and whizzes off through tubes called arteries to travel around your body. How does it know to go in the right direction, and not just back up into your lungs?

OPTION 1—GPS

OPTION 2—It leaves a trail of bread crumbs
so it can't get lost

OPTION 3—Valves

If you answered 1 or 2, go and sit in the corner for ten minutes. Blood goes in the right direction because there are valves in the heart that stop it from going backward and causing some kind of unpleasant blood-splattering explosion.

When all the oxygen has been delivered to your nose and your toes and your lips and your hips, the blood says a quick "Hi" and "Bye!" then heads straight off to collect

CIRCULATION

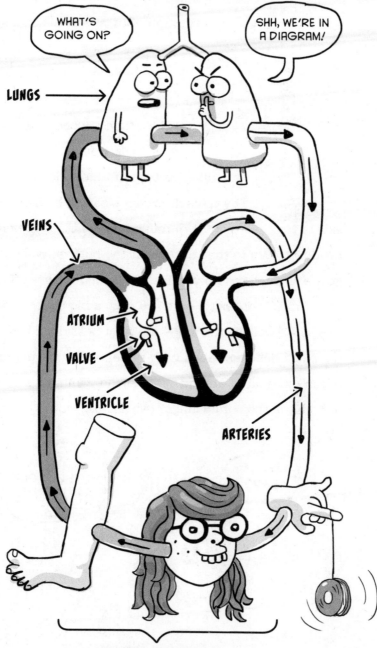

If you took all the arteries and veins in your body and laid them out end to end, they would stretch around the world about three times. Please don't do this—it would make a horrible mess, and I'm not cleaning up after you.

some more. It doesn't go back through your arteries, because the body uses a one-way system, like the kind grown-ups always moan about when they're driving. Blood that's on its way back travels through a different type of tube called a vein. The veins drop your blood off in the right side of your heart, again gurgling into the atrium before heading down to the ventricle at the bottom, where it gets a slightly less powerful squeeze and squirts off to your lungs. It doesn't have to be such a big squeeze on this side, because the lungs are right next door. When the blood has been filled with sweet, sweet oxygen, it doesn't just hang around there—who wants to waste their day in the boring lungs? (No offense, lungs.)

Instead, it pops back around to the left side of the heart. The blood in your body has now done a complete lap, but— unlike when you play *Mario Kart*—the heart can't rest for ten minutes and have a nice glass of milk; it immediately starts again with another pump. Nightmare.

No need to worry, though; your heart takes all this in stride. That's what the drumbeat is that you keep hearing, and will hear every moment for the rest of your life. Each beat is a squeeze of your heart, whooshing blood around your body. **BA-DUM. BA-DUM. BA-DUM.** Excuse me a second.

Will you shut up with that timpani please, Nigel? I'm trying to write a book here!

YOUR HEART RATE

But how does your heart know how often to beat?

Great question, me!

Thanks very much, me.

You're welcome, me.

Your heart is actually controlled by electricity. Luckily, it doesn't have a battery that can run out, so you never need to scrabble around trying to remember where you left your heart-charger. Instead, it uses the same kind of electricity as your TV or your vacuum or your robot butler.

WHY DID THEY PUT MY CHARGING PORT THERE?

This means that your body can send messages to your heart to tell it how slow or how fast to beat. If you're just sitting on the sofa watching *America's Most Boring Paint Colors* on TV, then your heart probably beats around eighty times a minute (a bit more than once a second). But if you decide to do something more energetic, like run around in the yard or play soccer or arm-wrestle a gorilla, then suddenly your leg and arm muscles need a lot more oxygen and the heart has to pump quicker to get it to them. So your heart rate goes up. Clever, right?

And just like your arm muscles get stronger from those constant arm-wrestling matches with gorillas, your heart muscle gets stronger with exercise.

BEFORE | AFTER

That's why when grown-ups tell you that it's a good idea to exercise, they're telling the truth for once. (A good form of exercise would be if you took Pippin out for a walk. Go on? Please? I promise she won't vomit then eat it all up again . . . much.) You need to keep your heart nice and strong because hopefully you agree by now that, as disgusting lumps of electrified muscle and blood go, it's pretty important.

While it would be extremely messy and dangerous for you to weigh your heart or find out how squishy it is, it's very safe and easy to tell how fast it's beating.

This is known as **TAKING YOUR PULSE**.

Because some arteries lie very close to your skin, you can feel the blood whooshing underneath, and each separate whoosh is a beat of the heart.

The easiest place to take your pulse is on your wrist. All you need is a watch (or a clock, or a timer on a phone) and a wrist. And a pulse, ideally.

TAKING YOUR PULSE

1 Hold out your left hand with the palm facing up, like you're hoping someone will drop a bar of chocolate into it. (You never know. . . .)

2 Press the index finger and the middle finger of your right hand (that's the two fingers next to your thumb, if you fell asleep during that lesson at school) onto your left wrist, just below the base of your thumb.

SO I'M NOT A ZOMBIE—I JUST NEED A BATH.

3 Press down a bit, and you can hopefully feel your pulse. If you can't, you might need to jiggle your fingers around a little or press harder. There it is!

4 Ask an adult if they know the name of the artery you're feeling. When they don't know the answer, you can tell them that it's the radial artery, and ask, "Did you even go to school?" Sorry if this results in you being sent to your bedroom for the next three years.

5 Now look at your watch for sixty seconds and count how many times your heart beats. Done!

If you can do all that, you're about a quarter of the way to becoming a fully qualified doctor. Congratulations.

Why don't you go for a run and see what your pulse is after that—it'll probably be a bit higher. Or you can try taking the pulse of your friends or your parents. Or your friends' parents. Or your friends' parents' friends. Don't try taking the pulse of your cat—it might scratch you. And I'm not entirely sure if cats even have wrists. (Oops, I shouldn't have written about cats—it's made Pippin go bananas.)

HEALTHY HEARTS

We need to be extra careful about looking after our heart—we've only got one. One each, I mean—we don't have one to share between all of us, like it's the class hamster. Besides exercising so it stays strong, there are a couple of other things you can do to keep your ticker ticking for as long as possible.

If your heart could speak, it would definitely tell you to eat healthy food. I know, I know—you don't want to eat your broccoli, and it's much more fun to munch your way through a bucket of popcorn the size of a traffic cone and a bar of chocolate as big as your front door. You can eat *some* of that stuff, but it has to be balanced out with things like fruit and vegetables. Why does your heart care about what you're eating? Surely that's the stomach's department. Well, if you eat too much unhealthy or fatty food for years and years and years, then when you're an adult some of the fat you've eaten can find its way into your arteries and gunk them up. Imagine playing a recorder—you blow through it, and the air flows out the other end, making a horrible noise. (You really should practice more.) Now imagine that someone has poured slime inside your recorder. It's much harder to blow through it, and the noise it makes is worse than ever. That's what happens when fat builds up inside your arteries—it's harder for the blood to get through, so it's harder for oxygen to get around your body.

When this happens, it's known as **CARDIOVASCULAR DISEASE**—cardiovascular is the fancy word for your heart and all your arteries and veins. There are a lot of long words in medicine—is that the first six-syllable word you've seen? Car-di-o-vas-cu-lar. (I can't imagine you've seen another one: that would be in-com-pre-hen-si-ble.)

Cardiovascular disease can stop you from doing things you enjoy, and that can make you unhappy, so it's best to get into the habit of exercising, saving treats for special times, and becoming better friends with Brussels sprouts. Other things that can cause cardiovascular disease include smoking and drinking too much alcohol. I don't want to ruin the rest of the book, but—spoiler alert—smoking and alcohol cause damage to *lots* of different parts of the body.

HOLE IN THE HEART

About one in every three hundred people is born with a hole in their heart—that means there's probably someone at your school who had one. No need to panic—the hole doesn't come out the front, spraying blood onto everyone they look at, like a firehose. The hole goes between the left and right halves, and means that blood with oxygen in it mixes with blood without oxygen and causes a bit of a muddle. Luckily, most of these holes are pretty small and close up on their own (your body can do this excellent magic trick of repairing itself), but some people need an operation, often before they're a year old. A baby's heart is the size of a strawberry, so fixing a tiny hole inside it means a pretty complex operation, and a very tiny needle and thread.

IF THE HEART STOPS

It's very, very serious if the heart stops beating, and anyone who that happens to needs urgent medical attention. It's possible to get the heart beating again using a machine called a defibrillator. You might have seen them on TV shows before—someone collapses, and the doctor puts a couple of pads on their chest, stands back, and says "CLEAR!" Then the patient splutters back to life. The defibrillator is actually giving the heart a bit of an electric shock, and because the heart beats using electricity (remember?), this can sometimes get it beating normally again.

If the heart stops beating but there's no defibrillator around, then it can also be helped by using something called CPR, or cardiopulmonary (*seven* syllables—a new record!) resuscitation. That means pressing on the chest to get the heart pumping, and sometimes blowing into the mouth of the person who has collapsed. Why don't you ask at school if they can arrange a class to teach you how to do CPR? (It's much more interesting than fractions, and you could literally save a life with it.)

TRANSPLANTS

A transplant is when an organ belonging to one person is very kindly donated to another person whose organ doesn't work anymore. For organs you have more than one of, like the kidneys, it's possible for a living person to donate one. But because you only have one heart and zombies aren't real (I hope), a heart can only be donated by someone who has died. The first heart transplant took place in 1967, and these days someone gets a heart transplant every two hours. (I mean different people do—it's not the same person getting loads of hearts.)

It takes about four hours to perform a heart transplant, so make sure you have a big breakfast if you plan on doing one any time soon. (I strongly recommend that you not perform any heart transplants unless you've been to medical school. Or, at the very least, watched a few YouTube videos about how to do them.)

The blue whale's heart is so big that you could stand up inside it. I recommend wearing a snorkel. There's a type of fruit fly with a heart the size of a grain of sand, which beats over 800 times a minute—good luck measuring its pulse!

HEART ATTACKS

Just like all the other organs in your body, your heart needs oxygen. Even though gallons of blood go through the middle of it, your heart doesn't actually get any of its own oxygen from that—it has a special supply from some blood vessels called the coronary arteries, which spider around the heart like . . . well, a spider. A heart attack is what happens if the coronary arteries get blocked so the heart doesn't get enough oxygen to be able to do its job.

If someone is having a heart attack, they often have pain that feels like an elephant is sitting on their chest, and sometimes also pain in their jaw, arm, or abdomen (that's the medical word for your tummy). It can cause sweating, sickness, or shortness of breath.

A heart attack is a very serious medical emergency, and if you see someone having one you need to call 911 immediately and ask for an ambulance.

KAY'S KWESTIONS

CAN YOU MAKE AN ARTIFICIAL HEART?

Yes! Well, not me personally. I'm no good at making stuff—I've spent three weeks trying to put up a shelf above my toilet, and it's still not

finished. But some clever scientists have made plastic artificial hearts, which can pump blood around the body. They cost as much as a Ferrari, so if you see one lying around don't step on it.

HOW MUCH BLOOD DOES THE HEART PUMP EVERY DAY?

Over seven thousand liters, which is enough to fill forty-four bathtubs to the brim with blood. (Please don't do this.)

HOW MANY TIMES WILL MY HEART BEAT IN MY LIFETIME?

Something like three and a half billion times, which is *loads*. That's more than the number of cats and dogs in the whole world. You don't just get a fixed amount of heartbeats before they all get used up and your heart stops. In fact, the more you make your heart beat fast with exercise, the longer it might last!

TRUE OR POO?

YOUR HEART STOPS WHEN YOU SNEEZE.

POO Lots of people think this is true, but actually it's totally made-up. If it were true, hospitals would be extremely full during allergy season.

YOUR HEART WAS YOUR VERY FIRST ORGAN TO DEVELOP.

TRUE Remember when you were the size of a jelly bean? No? Hmm. Me neither. Well, anyway, your heart started to appear right back then, ages before your lazy liver and slowpoke spine.

SOME PEOPLE HAVE THEIR HEARTS ON THE RIGHT SIDE OF THEIR BODY.

TRUE It's very rare, but it can happen. In fact, you'd have to do X-rays of ten thousand people before you found someone with their heart on the right (well, wrong) side. There's a complicated medical term for it: dextrocardia. As you'll soon find out, there's a complicated medical term for almost everything. I wonder who's in charge of naming all this stuff?

CHAPTER 3
BLOOD

LET'S TALK ABOUT the sticky, oozy, gloopy red liquid that's inside all of us. It's one of the few parts of your own innards that you ever get to see, so I thought you might want to know a few things about it.

There's a lot more to blood than just popping up to say hello if you cut yourself: it's your life juice—you can't live without it. I should point out that it's not *actual* juice— you really, really shouldn't be drinking it. (This doesn't apply to vampires—you guys can drink as much as you like, just don't have any of mine, please. Did I mention I had garlic sandwiches for lunch?)

WHAT BLOOD DOES

We know that blood is slurping all around inside us, but what does it actually do? The easiest way to think about

blood is like a transport system. You know those maps you see in train stations that show various lines disappearing off in different directions? Well, that's what blood does. And just like trains take all sorts of people around (miserable commuters with briefcases, tourists with massive backpacks that clonk into you, people eating smelly tuna sandwiches), blood takes all sorts of different things around your body. For example, oxygen needs to get everywhere—from your brain at the top to your bottom at the . . . bottom. Plus, your blood also carries the fuel that your body needs (known as nutrients), taking it from your digestive system (that's your stomach and intestines—nothing to do with cookies) to wherever it's required. And it also moves around any waste products that your cells produce, to get them out of the body. Unlike most train services, your

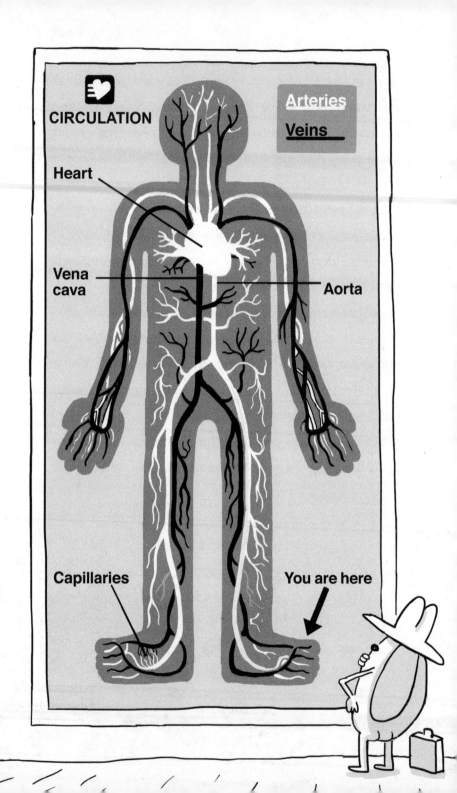

blood's always on the go—even when you're fast asleep. It also defends you from illnesses! So it's a postal service, a garbage-collection department, and a security guard. Oh, and it's a central-heating system too, working with its friend the skin so that your body is always that lovely 98.6 degrees. Plus, of course, it's a delicious snack. (Please ignore the last sentence if you're not a vampire.)

HOW BLOOD TRAVELS AROUND

You're not just a balloon filled with blood. I hope. Blood flows around your body using an incredible network called arteries and . . . Can you remember? Yep, that's right: arteries and BUTLERTRON-6000. No, hang on, that's the name of my robot butler. I meant arteries and veins.

ARTERIES

Arteries are the pipes that take blood full of oxygen from the heart to the rest of your body. The artery that comes straight out of the heart is called the **AORTA**, and it's the biggest artery of all. If it were a road, it would be a massive highway with ten lanes and those really big service stations with loads of restaurants and claw machines where you can win a soft toy. Almost immediately, the aorta branches off to smaller arteries, which branch off to even smaller arteries—these are more like the road you probably live on, with only a lane or two. The farther the arteries are from the heart, the smaller they get. By the time they reach your toes, they're really tiny—like narrow little paths a bicycle would barely fit on. Arteries have stretchy walls that can expand and shrink as the heart squirts blood through them, a bit like a hose that bulges out when the tap is turned all the way on.

I'M NOT A TOY!

VEINS

Veins are the other main type of blood vessel. Once the arteries have delivered oxygen, veins step in and take the used blood back to the heart. The veins start off tiny, like a stream that's so narrow the fish have to swim single file. But as they get closer and closer to the heart the veins get bigger and bigger, until they're more like massive rivers that hippos hang out in.

The biggest vein of all, which connects to the heart, is called the **VENA CAVA**. Vena cava is Latin for . . . hmm, I don't know that either—I was horrible at Latin. It probably means "massive vein" or something. I wish I hadn't started this paragraph now. Since blood doesn't whoosh through the veins as quickly as it does through the arteries, veins don't have to be as strong— their walls are thinner and a bit weak. (Please don't tell my veins I called them weak.)

Artery is the ancient Greek word for "contains air," because hundreds of years ago doctors thought that arteries were full of gas. Honestly, those guys were useless.

There's actually also a third type of blood vessel, called a **CAPILLARY**—I forgot about it because it's so small. A capillary is a tiny insect that eats leaves and then one day turns into a beautiful butterfly. Sorry, ignore me— that's a caterpillar. I read the wrong entry in the

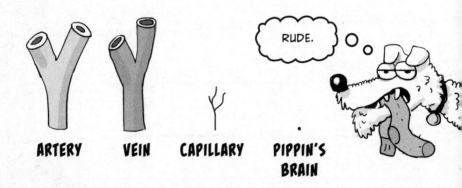

RUDE.

ARTERY   **VEIN**   **CAPILLARY**   **PIPPIN'S BRAIN**

dictionary. Capillaries are the tiniest type of blood vessel, and they sit between the arteries and the veins. The walls of capillaries are so thin that oxygen and fuel can pass straight through into the places that need them, like ghosts who can walk through walls. (Medical warning: don't try to walk through walls if you're not a ghost. I tried this morning and now I've got a really sore forehead.)

WHAT IS BLOOD MADE OF?

There are three types of blood cells: red blood cells, white blood cells, and platelets.

Platelets are a sort-of-kind-of yellow color, but for some reason they're not called sort-of-kind-of yellow blood cells. They're called platelets because they look a bit like little plates, which isn't very imaginative. I've heard there's some kind of naming committee in charge of all this—I'll try to find out a bit more about them.

All three kinds of cells swim around in a gross but important goo called plasma, which makes your blood nice and runny rather than a horrible sludge.

RED BLOOD CELLS

As the name suggests, they're red. In fact, they're the reason your blood has that ketchup-y color. They're the most common type of cell in your blood—in a single drop, there are over five million of them. (Five million is loads, by the way. That's the number of words you speak in two years if you're a real yabberer.) If you looked at red blood cells under a microscope, you'd see that they're round but slightly squished and flattened, like a gummy bear that you've accidentally sat on, or a beanbag that's lost most of its filling. Red blood cells carry all the oxygen around your body, and they can do that because they contain something called hemoglobin, which is like a backpack that stores oxygen.

Please sit down—I've got some sad news for you: red blood cells don't live forever. In fact, they get worn out and die after about four months. Oh, I thought you'd be more upset than that. How rude. Over their four-month life span, they travel about 300 miles around your body— that's the distance from Buckingham Palace to the Eiffel Tower. No wonder they're so exhausted. Luckily, you constantly produce new red blood cells to replace the ones that die, from a part of the body called the butt. Sorry, I wrote butt by accident—this chapter isn't going very well. I meant the bone marrow. Even though your bones are strong and hard, they've actually got a soft, squishy bit in the middle called the bone marrow, and this is where baby blood cells come from.

Bone marrow is the reason dogs find bones so delicious. Then again, Pippin also thinks sweaty socks are delicious, so you can't read too much into that.

Anyway, who knew bones weren't just there to keep you human-shaped but are also a disgusting Santa's workshop that makes blood? Ask your parents where red blood cells come from, and if they don't know, make them sit on the stairs for an hour in disgrace.

WHITE BLOOD CELLS

No prizes for guessing the color of white blood cells, but do you know what shape they are? Round? Square? Triangular? The shape of your math teacher's nose? Yep—all those answers are right. They're always changing shape, like they're made out of Play-Doh. You don't have as many white blood cells as you have of their red buddies, but they're just as important. They're the tough cookies in your body—the miniature army of superheroes who help you fight illness. Day in, day out, they patrol your body, looking for germs and other nasties that want to make you sick. There are different types of white blood cells, each designed to latch onto different types of germs. There are some for bacteria, some for viruses and some for worms. (Seriously! Your body has thought of *everything*.)

White blood cells are ruthless assassins—if they find something that shouldn't be there, they destroy it. While they're battling away, your white blood cells release chemicals into your bloodstream that cause your temperature to shoot up. They do this because a hotter body temperature makes it harder for germs to survive—so it's a good thing, I promise. (Even though it makes you feel like you're on a tropical beach at midday, wearing a thick wool sweater and toasting marshmallows on a massive fire.)

PLATELETS

Platelets work in teams, and their job is to help your blood to clot, which means to clump together into a big old lump. You obviously don't want your blood to do that while it's flowing around inside you, but if you have an accident and cut yourself, that's when platelets spring into action. Well, first they wait a moment, to give you time to scream about all the blood that's going everywhere. Then they make themselves all sticky and head over to plug the hole it's squirting out of. The bigger the cut, the more of their friends they call over to help out. And unlike my friends, who are always too busy sleeping or watching TV to reply to my messages, a platelet never leaves its buddies in the lurch.

PLASMA

Plasma sounds a lot more exciting than it actually is. Like it might be used in a laser gun or something. In fact, it's just the fluid that all the blood cells swim around in—and it looks suspiciously like pee. (I've checked with some scientists and they've promised me it definitely *isn't* pee.) Besides making blood its familiar, liquidy self, plasma also transports all the nutrients your body needs and carries hormones, which are the body's messaging system. (A bit like WhatsApp for cells—except hormones still work when the Wi-Fi's broken.)

IF YOU LOSE BLOOD

If you fall and cut your knee, your body is extremely good at replacing any blood you lose. It's a bit like when your robot butler runs low on batteries—you just plug him in and he's back to full power in no time at all. Usually when someone hurts themselves, the body can make more blood to replace what's lost, and everything is absolutely fine. But sometimes people lose a lot of blood in bad accidents or in very difficult operations, and the body can't replace it fast enough. Not having enough blood in your body is dangerous—you know by now how important blood is, especially for getting oxygen everywhere it's needed. But help is at hand. If you need a top-up, then you can have something called a blood transfusion.

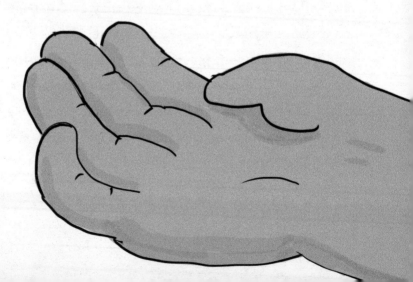

A blood transfusion is a very simple idea: you take a bag of blood and squirt it into a vein in someone's arm. And where does the blood come from? Other people! Relax—it's not stolen from them at night while they're asleep: they choose to donate it. You might have donated old toys or books to a charity shop before, and giving blood is exactly the same sort of thing. The main difference is you don't hand it over in an old trash bag. You go to a special donor center, where a nurse will hook you up to a tube that takes some blood out—about a couple of glasses' worth. You still have loads left, so a healthy person will feel totally fine after giving blood. After you've made your donation, they'll usually even give you a cookie. (I can't make any promises about what kind of cookie it will be, sorry.) But even better than the cookie is knowing that you've helped save someone's life. How

US hospitals need about 36,000 units of blood a day—that's enough to fill a really big swimming pool. (It would be a waste of blood sloshing it all into a swimming pool, so they give it to patients who need it instead.)

often can you say you've done that? Probably not often at all. Unless you're Batman, obviously. (If you *are* Batman, can I borrow your car, please? It looks much more fun than mine.)

You'll have to wait until you're seventeen before you can give blood, but please think about doing it then—it's an amazing gift to give someone in need.

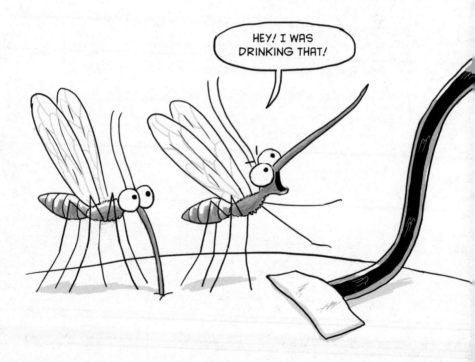

HEY! I WAS DRINKING THAT!

BLOOD TYPES

Cows have more than 800 different blood types, so this chapter would be very long if I were writing a book for cows. (I'd probably call it *Cows' Anatomy*.)

Different people have different types of blood. It's just like the way people have different-colored eyes or different-length tongues, or how some people are good at writing books (me) and other people are absolutely terrible at it (my brothers).

When doctors give someone a blood transfusion, it's very important to know the patient's blood type, because some blood types don't get along at all (like my brothers won't get along with me when they read that last paragraph), and it would make the person who received the wrong kind of blood very ill. The four blood types are A, B, AB, and O. (You can remember them as apples, bananas, and oranges. Or you can just remember them normally—it's not that hard, come on.) O is a very special blood type because absolutely anyone in the world can get a transfusion of type O blood. It's like a person who's extremely easy to get along with, such as . . . you! (Ignore that if you're actually horrible.)

KAY'S KWESTIONS

WHY ARE SCABS HARD IF THEY'RE MADE OF BLOOD?

Remember platelets—rushing to the scene of a cut like tiny plate-shaped paramedics and doing their sticky thing to stop

the blood from pouring out? Well, after they've done that, they leave a mesh of fibrin, which is a very strong material that forms the scabs you know and love. Next time a grown-up yells at you to stop picking a scab, you can tell them that it's actually a mesh of fibrin. But they're right—you shouldn't pick it. It's there to keep germs from coming in, and to protect your skin while it repairs itself. Once the skin has healed, the scab (sorry, I mean mesh of fibrin) will fall off by itself.

IF MY BLOOD IS RED, THEN WHY ARE MY VEINS BLUE?

Your veins are actually red—they just look blue on the outside. It's an optical illusion because of the way light gets absorbed by your skin. No humans have blue blood . . . though spiders, crabs, and squids do. This is because they don't carry oxygen using hemoglobin—their blood uses hemocyanin, which is blue. (Bonus fact: worms have green blood!)

WHY DO SOME PEOPLE FAINT AT THE SIGHT OF BLOOD?

Because it's disgusting. Oh, you want a more scientific answer? Okay, fine. If you start to panic about something, your brain sends a message along a nerve (the vagus nerve, if you're taking notes) to try to calm you down. One of the effects of this is to slow your heart down. Sometimes it makes your heart slow down a little bit *too* much, and then suddenly it's . . . *clonk*—hello, floor! It's nothing to be embarrassed about—it happens to lots and lots of people. In fact, it happened to me a few times when I was at medical school . . . I once fainted when I was sewing up a cut on a man's arm. Oops! Luckily, I didn't cut my head and need to be sewn up myself. (By the way, someone else came along to help the man out. He's not still sitting there, bleeding all over the floor.)

TRUE OR POO?

LEECHES ARE USED BY DOCTORS TODAY.

TRUE Hundreds and hundreds of years ago, doctors didn't really understand how the body worked, so they came up with some unusual (and completely useless) treatments. One particular favorite in the olden days was using leeches to treat anything from heart problems to infected legs. Leeches are like ugly slugs with a massive mouth containing three hundred teeth, and

THIS IS GOING TO TAKE AGES.

they suck your blood. Doctors stopped using leeches a long time ago (mainly because they killed quite a lot of patients), but these days they've made a bit of a reappearance: surgeons use them to help blood flow in the area they're operating on. Leeches can eat ten times their weight in blood during a single meal. That's like you eating about two thousand hamburgers at lunch. (Please don't do this.)

YOUR BLOOD CONTAINS GOLD.

TRUE Blood contains small amounts of metals, such as iron, copper, and gold. Don't get too excited, though—it really is a very tiny amount. You would need to take every drop of blood out of all the people in a full football stadium to collect enough gold to make a small ring. (Please don't do this or I'll have to call the police.)

ONE IN TEN PEOPLE NEEDS A BLOOD TRANSFUSION DURING THEIR LIFE.

POO In fact, over half of all people need a blood transfusion at some point. All the more reason to give blood—it's a fair swap if you might need someone else's one day, don't you think?

BREATHE IN. BREATHE OUT. Breathe in, breathe out. Is there anything more to the lungs than that? I certainly hope so, because I've got to write an entire chapter about them. So sit down, take a deep breath, and let's find out everything there is to know about your airbags.

Breathing—or respiration, if we're going to be fancy about it—is all about getting oxygen into your tissues. Not the kind of tissues that you sneeze into (although more about that later), I mean all the different bits of your body. Oxygen is what keeps them, and you, alive. The things you do every day, like moving, eating, thinking, and farting, are only possible because of O (oxygen).

Breathing is a two-way process: you breathe in fresh air and breathe out not-so-fresh air. The breathing-in part is called **inspiration**. (I don't mean like when you're inspired by a singer or a sports star, or someone who can eat two hundred doughnuts in an hour.) After the oxygen has been packed off around the blood, the remaining air has to come out, and in place of the oxygen that's used up, there's another gas called carbon dioxide (or CO_2 to its friends). Breathing out is also known as **expiration**. (I don't mean like the expiration date on those doughnuts.)

INSIDE YOUR LUNGS

Open wide—it's time to find out how breathing works. Air rushes in through your mouth (that big thing you can't keep shut) or your nose (that big thing you keep sticking your fingers into). It then goes into your throat, which is a double agent—it's where both air and food make their grand entrance, before going into either the esophagus (food) or the trachea (air). It's important that everything go down the correct tube, so you've got a little lid on the top of your trachea called the epiglottis, which directs everything exactly where it should go, like a slimy crossing guard. It doesn't get everything right

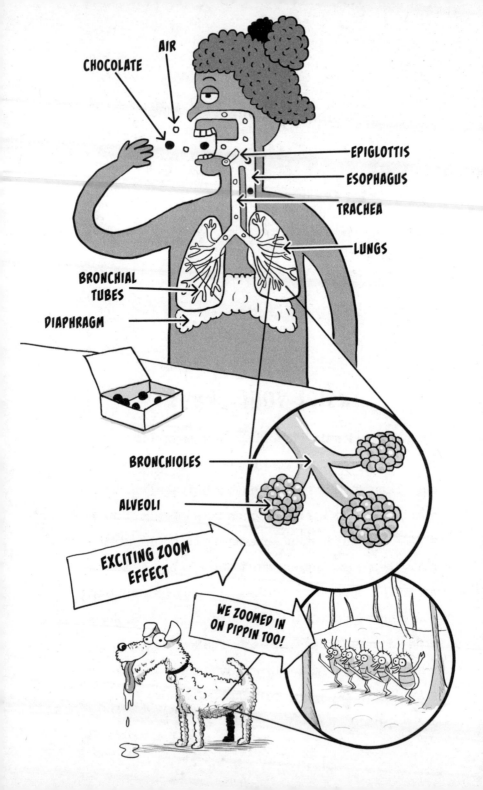

100 percent of the time. (Who does? Oh, really—*you* do? Let me just check with your teacher. . . .) Next time some food goes down the wrong hole, you can say, "Due to an error with my epiglottis, food has traveled into my trachea instead of my esophagus." Once you've stopped coughing, that is.

So the air goes down your trachea, which is also known as your windpipe. (I don't know why it gets called that— the esophagus isn't known as your lunchpipe.) The trachea divides into two bronchial tubes, and one of those goes into each of your butt cheeks. Sorry, lungs.

Your lungs are pink, rubbery, and the size of . . . well, feel your ribs—they're that size. They're not identical: the left one is smaller and made up of two sections (called lobes) and the right one is a bit bigger and made of three lobes. This is because your heart is nestled in with your left lung and it's all tightly packed in there like a squishy 3D jigsaw puzzle.

The bronchial tubes start out the width of your finger and then divide into smaller and smaller pipes, until they reach the bronchioles, which are the width of a mouse's finger. These tubes are all known as your airways (and, if you're British, they're known as your British airways). At the end of your bronchioles are alveoli, which are tiny bags of air, like microscopic Bubble Wrap. They're not to be confused with ravioli, which are little square parcels of pasta that taste a lot better than alveoli. If you spread out all your alveoli on the ground, they would cover the area of a tennis court. I very strongly recommend that you not do this, however, because they're pretty crucial bits of your lungs: they're the parts that grab the oxygen and get it into your bloodstream, ready for your heart to pump it around your body. At the same time, your alveoli also take carbon dioxide out of your bloodstream and whoosh it back up your bronchioles so it can skedaddle out of there: it's basically the poop of your lungs. It's a very efficient system—and it all happens in, well, the time it takes you to breathe in and out.

Because your breath has been in your body, it comes out at body temperature—a sizzling 98.6 degrees. That means when it's cold outside and you breathe onto a window, the glass will steam up. It's the law that you then have to either write your name in it, or draw something disgusting with your finger (if there's nobody around to yell at you).

Breathing is one of those things that, like your heart beating, happens in the background without you having to think about it—a bit like a driverless car, or when your robot butler does your homework for you. (Honestly, you *really* should get one.)

Your brain constantly monitors the levels of oxygen and carbon dioxide in your body so it can tell your lungs if they need to get pumping any harder. It's just as well you don't have to think about breathing, because you do it every few seconds, which is at least twenty thousand times a day, so you wouldn't have much time to think about anything else. And, like every other part of your body, the lungs can't move without your muscles lending a . . . well, not a hand. Your muscles don't have hands. Without your muscles lending a muscle.

The big boss breathing muscle is your diaphragm. There are three things you need to know about the diaphragm: it's shaped like a dome, it sits under your lungs, and that G in its name is totally unnecessary. Apparently the head of the naming committee is a man named Clive— I might write to him to find out why it's there.

When your body decides you should breathe in, your diaphragm moves downward and becomes a lot flatter. It's a team player, so at the same time, loads of little muscles between your ribs (called intercostal muscles) make your rib cage push outward. This all causes the lungs to get bigger, which means that air is sucked in.

When it's time to get rid of your manky old lung-poop (or carbon dioxide, if you're writing about it in an exam), then the reverse happens: the diaphragm pushes back up into a dome shape and the ribs pull back in, and this makes the lungs get smaller. It's exactly the same as what happens if you take a full balloon, untie the knot, then push in the sides—all the air whooshes out (and you get kicked out of the birthday party).

MUCUS

This is a whole section on mucus. If you don't want to read a whole section on mucus, you should probably skip to the next part. But, mucus lovers, strap in—this part is especially for you.

Mucus, or phlegm (*what's with all these unnecessary Gs?*), is a slimy, jellylike liquid that lives inside your lungs. It might not win any beauty contests, but your mucus has got a very important job to do: keeping your lungs nice and clean. Its sticky sliminess is absolutely perfect for trapping any dust or germs that might have sneaked down into your airways. When mucus has caught some gunk, it slides upward, mucus-ing its way toward your mouth using tiny hairs on the inside of your bronchial tubes. (Oh yeah, sorry. Just in case you haven't been put off your dinner yet, your lungs are full of tiny hairs. Maybe book an extra ten minutes next time you're at the hairdresser's?)

When the mucus gets to the top of your windpipe, sometimes your throat goes "Absolutely not—no way!" and coughs it out. But more often, you swallow your mucus without even being aware of it. You're probably doing it now. Nothing to be alarmed about— just a constant trail of delicious mucus sliding up your windpipe and down into your stomach. Yum!

Your lungs produce over a liter of mucus every day. That's enough to fill three cans of baked beans. When you cough, it travels at roughly fifty miles per hour, which is about twice as quick as the fastest sprinters in the world, or ten times as quick as Pippin. She's so lazy.

SMOKING

I'm sure you already know that smoking is bad for you. But it's not just bad for you. It's *really* bad for you. In fact, it's one of the most harmful things you can possibly do to your body. Why is it legal, then? That's a very good question (well done, me), but I don't exactly know the answer (not so well done, me). Maybe it shouldn't be legal.

Your lungs have a built-in lubrication system so that breathing is a smooth, sliding delight rather than a creaky, crunchy nightmare. They sit inside a balloon of slime called pleural fluid, which helps them expand easily with every breath. It works a bit like a waterslide—imagine trying to hurtle down one if there were no water flowing. You wouldn't hurtle at all, would you? You'd get stuck on all the bends. Worst water park ever.

Smoking affects your lungs and airways in lots of different ways, and it's *never* an upgrade. You've just read how mucus is important for kicking out any nasties that have found their way into your tubes. If you smoke, it damages the little hairs that lift the mucus up and out of the lungs, so mucus gets trapped inside. This means smokers are much more likely to get lung infections, because germs can't get booted out of their lungs. It's also why smokers have that grim, hacking cough that sounds like Pippin sicking up her dinner.

We'll talk more about cancer later, but as I'm sure you already know, it's not a good thing to have. It means that some cells in the body have grown abnormally, and it can be life-threatening. You'd think that people wouldn't deliberately do things that make cancer more likely, but that's exactly what smoking does. And it doesn't just cause lung cancer—it can lead to at least fifteen different types of cancer.

Another thing: cigarette smoke contains carbon monoxide, which is a poison. An actual, literal poison that makes it much harder for your blood to carry oxygen. Why on earth would you want to make it harder for your blood to carry oxygen? Even my dog understands how important that is (and she thinks that door handles are alive and woofs every time she walks past one).

Smoking also damages the walls of your alveoli, so you feel out of breath all the time. But stick around—it gets worse. Cigarettes have tar in them, the same sticky stuff that you make roads with, and—surprise!—that's also poisonous. And it's not just your lungs that suffer from being filled with goo. Tar and other chemicals affect every single blood vessel in your body, making them narrower and putting strain on your heart. Plus, smoking weakens your bones, wrinkles your skin, and squashes your sense of taste. Have I put you off yet? Oh, and it gives you bad breath, teeth like old stones (seriously— Pippin has nicer teeth), and a furry yellow tongue like a dead caterpillar.

There is one bit of good news, though. As soon as someone stops smoking, things quickly return to normal. Their sense of taste comes back within a couple of days, and after a month or two the little hairs that protect the lungs will repair themselves and get on with their job of filtering out the nasties. But much better than stopping smoking is never starting in the first place.

POLLUTION

You know all about pollution—the muck that spews out of cars and factories and planes, heating up the world and melting the ice caps. (Actually, you probably know more about that stuff than me—I'm just the medicine guy.) But pollution isn't just bad for penguins and polar bears, it's bad for us humans too.

Pollution means that the air is full of tiny bits of dirt, and—you guessed it—this dastardly dust finds its way into our lungs. These little flecks are so small that they can escape the body's natural defenses and cause you to cough and get short of breath. If you already have a condition that affects your lungs, like asthma, then pollution can make it much worse.

STINK INC

You breathe in enough air a day to fill about a thousand balloons. Unless we're talking hot-air balloons, that is. It would take you about half a year to inflate one of those just using your breath, and you've probably got better things to do.

And—sorry, I don't really have any good news for you here—breathing in pollution can have long-term effects on your heart and lungs. It's time for us to stop climbing into cars and get our butts on bikes instead.

ASTHMA

Asthma is the most common lung condition in the world—if you don't have it yourself, then I'm sure you know people who do. If you don't know anyone who does, then you probably live on your own in a swamp in the middle of an abandoned forest, because more than 25 million people in the US alone have asthma.

Asthma doesn't make it hard to breathe all the time—it comes and goes—but when it shows its face this is known as a flare-up or an asthma attack. During an asthma attack, your airways swell, which means it's harder for air to get into your lungs. Next time you've got a straw, try taking a breath through it—you'll see it's much harder to breathe through a smaller hole: that's what asthma attacks are like. Now stop breathing through the straw and get back to your milkshake. Asthma can make your chest feel tight, cause you to cough, or give your breath a whistling sound known as wheezing.

I can't tell you what causes asthma in the first place (this isn't just me being useless—nobody knows), but it runs in families, and often affects people who also have other conditions, like eczema and allergies. People with asthma sometimes have things called **TRIGGERS** that make it flare up—that might mean dust, pollen, or animal hair. If that's the case for you, then you might need to do things like change your sheets more regularly, have wooden floors instead of carpets, stay inside when the pollen count is high, and avoid animal hair. This means doing things like not letting animals into your bedroom—you don't need to shave your pets. Pippin just woofed a sigh of relief.

Other triggers include exercise, cold weather, perfume, and eating mushrooms. (Eating mushrooms is never a trigger, actually. When I was growing up, I just always wished there were a page in a textbook I could point to, to prove to my mom that I shouldn't have to eat mushrooms. And now you have such a page to show annoying grown-ups. Don't let them see this bit in parentheses, though.)

Asthma is usually treated with inhalers—I'm sure you've seen people using them at school before. There are lots of different types of inhaler—for example, the blue one that widens the airways if you're having a flare-up and the brown one that you use every day to prevent flare-ups in the first place. Then there's the big gold-colored one that bends in an S-shape and is covered in buttons and gets wider at the end. . . . No, hold on, that's a saxophone.

Asthma doesn't stop you from living your life. Famous athletes such as David Beckham, Jerome Bettis, and Kristi Yamaguchi all have asthma, and so does the most handsome man in the world (me).

COLLAPSED LUNG

Just like a bicycle tire can spring a leak, the same thing can happen to one of your lungs. This is called a pneumothorax, which is quite a complicated word, so most of us just call it a collapsed lung. We don't really know why lungs decide to collapse, but it happens mainly to tall, thin boys. Perhaps it's revenge for them being good at basketball? A collapsed lung makes it difficult to breathe and causes sudden pain in one side of the chest, and it generally requires a trip to the hospital. Unlike a tire, this can't be fixed with a rubber patch and a bicycle pump. Sometimes a collapsed lung gets better on its own, sometimes you need an oxygen mask, and sometimes (stop reading this sentence immediately if you're squeamish) doctors need to stick a needle into your chest to remove the air that has leaked out of your lung.

STETHOSCOPE

If you go to the doctor with a breathing-based issue, they'll probably have a listen to your chest with a stethoscope. (In fact, if they don't, maybe you should ask to see their medical certificate or check the sign on the door—it's possible you've wandered into a fishmonger's by mistake.) You know the stethoscope—it's that Y-shaped gadget with a couple of earpieces and a long tube that connects to a disc at the other end. Doctors use it to listen to the lungs for any wheezing that might indicate asthma, or any crackles that might mean there's an infection brewing. It can also be used to listen to the heart, or the tummy, or any parts of the body that make interesting noises. (Apart from *that* one.)

KAY'S KWESTIONS

HOW LONG CAN WE HOLD OUR BREATH?

Not that long, really—somewhere between thirty seconds and a minute. Any longer than that and it gets dangerous because your body doesn't like carbon dioxide building up in the blood—too much of it and you'll faint. If you're reading this and you're a blue whale, then the answer is you can hold your breath for an hour and a half. This is extremely useful if one of your relatives lets off a particularly noxious fart. (Yes, whales do fart, I checked. I'm not sure what whale farts smell like, but I'm guessing . . . not great?)

> I might have to take my laptop to a shop to repair the   key, I mean the   key, I mean the Q key if it doesn't get better soon.

DO YOU NEED BOTH LUNGS?

Some people live quite happily with just one lung, and you'd never know. (Unless you saw the big scar going halfway around their chest.) It's not common to remove a lung, but it can happen after a bad injury, or as part of treatment for lung cancer. Pope Francis had a lung removed as a teenager and it hasn't stopped him from doing any of his . . . pope-ing?

WHAT ARE HICCUPS?

Hiccups are caused by little twitches in your diaphragm that suck air really quickly down your windpipe. *Hic!* They sometimes happen if you've eaten food too fast or had too many fizzy drinks. *Hic!* Sometimes they happen if you're nervous or excited . . . but often they happen for no reason at all. They normally disappear on their own, but some people find that their hiccups go away if they hold their breath (not for too long, though; otherwise you'll have bigger problems than hiccups). Very rarely, hiccups don't go away on their own and you might need to take medicine to get rid of them. One man, named Charles Osborne, hiccupped constantly for sixty-eight years, which must have really annoyed his family. *Hic! Hic! Hic!*

TRUE OR POO?

ASTRONAUTS BREATHE PEE.

TRUE There isn't any oxygen in space, so astronauts on the International Space Station need to make it themselves. It's not too tricky getting oxygen from water—H_2O (the chemical formula for water) splits neatly into H (hydrogen) and O (oxygen). But since grocery stores don't deliver bottled water to space, astronauts need to find other sources on board. Such as . . . pee. It's not quite as bad as it sounds—the pee gets purified first. Even so, yuck.

YOU CAN SWALLOW AND BREATHE AT THE SAME TIME.

POO Because of your epiglottis—remember, that little flap over your trachea—you can either swallow or breathe at any one time, but never both. The epiglottis snaps shut if it gets so much as a whiff of a Pringle.

YOUR LUNGS WOULD FLOAT ON WATER.

TRUE Your lungs are in fact the only organ in your body that can float, thanks to all their air-filled ravioli. Sorry, alveoli. Whichever scientist found this out must have spent a particularly messy day dropping organs into a swimming pool.

CHAPTER 5

BRAIN

I DON'T KNOW how often you stop and think about your brain, but if you ever do stop and think about your brain . . . it's your brain that's doing all the thinking about itself. Weird, right? If you've never thought about it before, here are the basics: your brain is a supercomputer that sits inside your skull and controls pretty much everything you do. It's more powerful than any computer on Earth—in fact, it's made up of 100 trillion different connections. It's hard to describe how big 100 trillion is: it's the number of stars in a thousand galaxies. If you had 100 trillion dollars, you could buy every single house on the planet. If someone started counting on the first day the Earth existed, they still wouldn't have gotten up to 100 trillion yet. What I'm saying is the brain is really, really, *really* amazing. Even *your* brain, which sometimes forgets to tell you to brush your teeth.

If you're feeling a bit peckish, so you pick your nose, or you decide you don't like your brother, so you lock him in the bathroom, or you've had enough of a book (not this one, obviously) and chuck it across a room, that's your brain doing its job: bossing the rest of your body around. The craziest thing about the brain is that even though scientists have been studying it for thousands of years, there's still loads we don't know—it's very secretive and likes to keep its mysteries to itself. I'll be honest: this makes it slightly tricky writing an entire chapter about it. But I'll work out something to say—I'll just use my . . . oh, that's right, brain.

I don't know if you've ever taken your brain out and weighed it, but it's about three pounds—that's the same as four iPads. The reason it's all wrinkled is just to cram as much brain in there as possible. If it was all unfolded, it would be about as big as your pillow. (Once again—and I can't emphasize this enough—please don't unfold your brain to check if it's pillow-sized. The last thing I need right now is a load of grown-ups complaining to me that their pillowcases have been ruined by brain juice.)

THE BITS OF THE BRAIN

You know how in cartoons brains look like squishy, freaky, wrinkly lumps of horror? Well, I'm thrilled to be able to tell you that the cartoons are pretty accurate.

The main part of the brain—the part that looks like a folded-up chain of sausages gone wrong—is the cerebrum. It's divided into left and right halves, and one weird thing is that each half controls the opposite side of your body. So for example, your right brain looks after your left nostril and your left elbow, and your left brain looks after your right ankle and your right butt cheek.

The cerebrum is divided into lots of different lobes. That's a weird word, isn't it? Lobes. Lobes, lobes, lobes. Like globes but without the G. Stop distracting me, brain—where was I? Oh, that's right. Each of the lobes has different jobs. I mean, it's fair enough—there's a lot of stuff for the brain to be arranging, so it splits up the work. (Like when your teacher makes you all clean up the classroom because they can't be bothered to.)

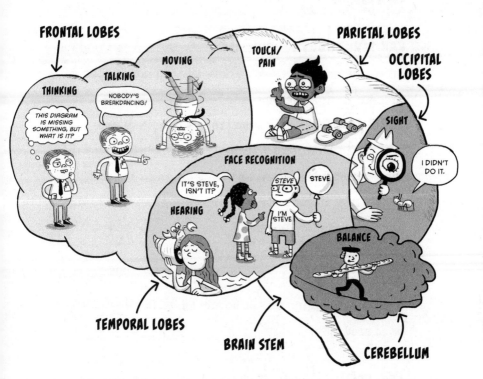

FRONTAL LOBES — These are the lobes at the front of the brain. (Clive and his naming committee weren't very imaginative with this one.) They're in charge of thinking, talking, and moving—so, pretty important.

TEMPORAL LOBES — These are at the sides, underneath the parts of your head called the temples. (Again, bit of a lazy name, Clive.) The temporal lobes look after hearing and recognizing things like people's faces. This is quite handy; otherwise, every morning when you came down to breakfast you'd see a bunch of total strangers.

PARIETAL LOBES — (Whoa! Clive's just started making up words now.) These sit above the temporal lobes and process things like pain and touch.

OCCIPITAL LOBES — These are at the back of your brain and are in charge of your sight. It's slightly weird that the occipital lobes are at the back and not near your eyes. Maybe your body read the "How to make a brain" instructions in reverse.

There are a few other parts of the brain that hang out with the cerebrum and its lovely lobes. Some important ones are:

CEREBELLUM — This is a wrinkly walnut at the bottom of your brain that helps with your balance. (I mean it looks like a walnut—it's not actually a walnut.)

BRAINSTEM — If you think of your cerebrum as a strange, disgusting gray flower, then the brain stem is the stem underneath it. It looks after involuntary actions, which are the things you don't even think about. Breathing, for instance. Whoops, I've made you think about breathing now, haven't I? In a minute, when you've stopped thinking about breathing, the brain stem will have you covered. Plus, it keeps your heart beating, and sorts out anything else you do without thinking, like when your mouth waters because you see a slice of chocolate cake or some fox poop (if you're Pippin). Another thing your brain stem handles is the fight-or-flight response. This happens when your body senses danger—for instance, if you wake up and there's a lion in your bedroom. Your brain makes the decision whether to stay there and face it (fight) or run away as quickly as possible (flight—I recommend this option). It's why your heart beats faster and you breathe quicker when you're scared—your brain stem has decided to get as much oxygen as possible into your body, in case your leg muscles need to make a speedy exit!

HIPPOCAMPUS — Nothing to do with hippos, I'm afraid. Or camping, for that matter. (What was Clive thinking?!) The hippocampus helps you with your memories. So if you remember seeing a hippo or going camping, then that's thanks to your hippocampus.

HYPOTHALAMUS — Hungry? Thirsty? Sleepy? That's your hypothalamus pulling the strings. I don't mean literally—you're not a puppet.

BLOOD–BRAIN BARRIER — Because your brain is extremely important, it stops anything dangerous or poisonous from sneaking into it through the bloodstream. This is thanks to the blood–brain barrier, which is like a magic invincibility cloak that goes all the way around the brain. It was discovered over a hundred years ago by a scientist who injected purple dye into the bloodstream of animals (*AAAAGH!*) and noticed that every organ in their bodies turned purple (*AAAAGH! again*) apart from the brain, which made him realize there was some kind of barrier there.

AMYGDALA — I'm sure you've never gotten angry. Not you. No way—don't be ridiculous. But if you ever *did* get angry, then it would be your amygdala making it happen, so feel free to blame any future tantrums on your amygdala. Besides making you angry, it's also in charge of making you feel afraid, so your amygdala will be working overtime if a zombie ever steals your chips.

YOUR NERVOUS SYSTEM

Not nervous like "Uh-oh, a tiger's charging toward me and for some reason I'm wearing pants made entirely out of raw meat" or nervous like "Uh-oh, it's my very important exams next week but, instead of studying, I made a life-sized model of Harry Styles out of earwax and drew emojis on my sneakers." It's called the nervous system because it's a system made up of all your nerves. Nerves are skinny little wires that transmit electrical signals to and from your brain and, like your blood vessels, they have to reach *everywhere*.

If your brain wants to get your body to do anything, then chances are it needs to

If your parents say that you're getting on every inch of their nerves, you can tell them that their bodies contain about six billion inches of nerves in total. (Warning: this might make them even more annoyed with you.)

119

send a message down your spinal cord. Your spine is the knobbly, bony thing in your back that runs from your brain to your butt, and in the middle of it is a big old bundle of nerves about as thick as your finger, called the spinal cord. (If you rearrange all the letters in "spinal cord," you get "rancid slop"—please never describe your food as this to a chef.) Once the message has made its way down the spinal cord, it pings off to your peripheral nerves.

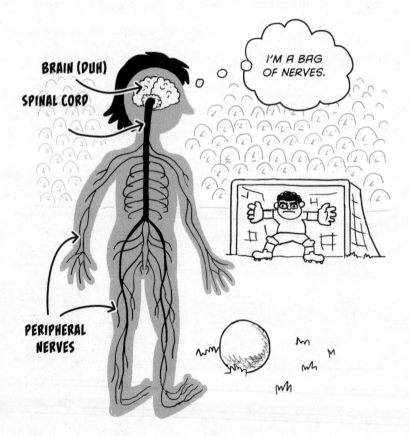

PERIPHERAL NERVES are any nerves that aren't in your brain or spinal cord, and they get messages to and from whichever corner of your body they need to. If you want to stick out your tongue or wave your hand, that's a peripheral nerve (or twelve) that you're using. Your peripheral nerves are made up of different fibers, just like how an electrical cable has a few different wires inside it. (*Please* don't cut up the wire going into your TV to check—that would be dangerous, and worse still, you wouldn't be able to watch TV anymore.) Some fibers send messages away from the spinal cord to move parts of your body, and other ones send messages in the opposite direction to report back to your brain.

So if you decide you want to wiggle your toe . . . the frontal lobe in the cerebrum of your brain sends a message to the bottom of your spinal cord, which passes the message on to a peripheral nerve called the sciatic nerve, which goes all the way down your leg and passes it on to another peripheral nerve called the peroneal nerve, and then ta-da! One wiggling toe! If you weren't concentrating while you were wiggling, your toe might touch a cactus. A nerve would then send the cactus-y news back up different fibers of those nerves to your spinal cord, which would ping it straight up to your brain (the parietal lobe, in fact) to tell you that it was painful. Ouch! Maybe don't do any toe-wiggling near cacti in the future?

If you're wondering how all those steps happen so quickly, well, your nerves are extremely fast. They send messages at 250 miles per hour—which is over three times the highway speed limit, so I hope there weren't any traffic police watching you wiggle your toe just then.

If you put any living thing under a microscope and zoom right in, you'll see cells. (If you zoom in on a prison you'll see cells too, but they're not quite the same.) There are loads of types of cells—they're all tiny and they all do different things. Your skin is made of skin cells. Your blood is made of blood cells. And your brain is made of . . . Nope! Neurons. Go sit in a puddle for half an hour. Neurons are my favorite type of cell (don't tell the kidney cells, or they'll get upset) because . . . well, they just look the best, like wild alien cells. And some neurons are massive—a single cell can stretch down your entire arm or leg!

You might think cells are tiny, but an ostrich egg is a cell that's the length of a pencil!

DIFFERENT PEOPLE'S BRAINS

ADHD

You or one of your friends might have a condition called ADHD, which stands for attention deficit hyperactivity disorder. That means it can be harder, or completely impossible, to sit still or concentrate in class. Sometimes it can mean that people appear absentminded and they have trouble remembering things. We each look different, so it makes sense that we each have different types of brains. Lots of extremely successful people have ADHD, including Justin Timberlake (famous singer), Simone Biles (Olympic gold medalist), and Walt Disney (I think he made cartoons or something).

AUTISM

You might also know about autism. It's a condition that affects people in all sorts of ways, some more than others. Autistic people can often find it harder to meet strangers or make friends, or to understand how others think or feel. Sometimes they don't communicate emotion very well, or they might not get jokes, and they like to do the same things every day. It doesn't mean they're less clever—autistic people can be brilliant in a wide range of subjects. Like absolutely everyone, there are some things in life they're better at and some things they're less good at.

EPILEPSY

People with epilepsy have seizures. This can mean that they fall down and shake all over, or that a certain part of their body moves around, or that they stop and stare for a few minutes or begin stammering. Seizures don't happen all the time—in fact, someone with epilepsy might only have a seizure once every few months, or even less than that. Epilepsy is a condition in which neurons in the brain get overexcited and send out signals when they shouldn't. People with epilepsy can take medicine to stop this from happening. If you see someone having a seizure, try not to leave them alone, but if there isn't an adult nearby, then you should go and get help from a grown-up as quickly as possible.

DYSLEXIA

A lot of people have trouble with reading and writing, and sometimes they need extra assistance at school. In many cases it's nothing to do with intelligence—it's a condition called dyslexia, which affects how the brain processes the letters it sees and turns them into words. Some of the most successful people in the history of the world have been dyslexic—your friends with dyslexia could become singers like John Lennon, film directors like Steven Spielberg, or presidents like George Washington. Just to be extra confusing, there are a couple of other conditions that start with "dys" and end with "ia" where your brain works slightly differently. **DYSCALCULIA** means you have difficulties with numbers, and **DYSPRAXIA** is a condition that affects your coordination, which means the way all your different muscles work together.

SLEEP

There are two types of people in the world: those who love their duvet and would happily snore away until lunchtime, and those who think sleep is *boring* and would rather drink a warm cup of vomit than go to bed. (I'm in team snore-a-thon. In fact, I'm typing this sentence from bed.) But, like it or not, we all have to sleep. Sleep is extremely important—it's how your body recharges. After a hard day's walking around or smashing up skyscrapers (if you're Godzilla), you have to give muscles some time out, and your brain needs a rest too.

Even when you're fast asleep and your body is in stand-by mode, your brain is still working away, just at a more chilled-out pace. It sorts through all the things you've seen and done that day and decides whether they're important memories it should store away (for example, what you learned at school) or a load of nonsense that it should throw out (like a YouTube video of a goat sneezing). Or maybe that should be the other

The longest anyone has ever stayed awake is just over eleven days! It was Randy Gardner, a student, who did this from the end of 1963 to 1964 at age seventeen. He must have been so grumpy afterward.

way around. Scientists think that's what dreams are—your brain is basically scrolling really fast through the Instagram feed of everything your eyes saw that day. I say they *think* that's what dreams are because no one really knows for sure. Maybe you'll be the person to find out. Don't forget to mention how brilliant I am in your speech if you get a Nobel Prize.

One thing we do know is that there are five different stages of sleep, from really light sleep, where you'd wake up if a fly farted, all the way to deep sleep, which it's much harder to wake from. Dreams happen in a stage of snoozing called REM (rapid eye movement) sleep, because your eyes dart all over the place like you're watching a tennis match on fast-forward. You're really not yourself if you don't get enough sleep—it means it's harder to concentrate and learn new things, and it makes you really grouchy. (Not just you—it makes everyone really grouchy. Wait, sorry—your parents just emailed me. It does make *you* especially grouchy.) So go to bed! Actually, finish this chapter first.

MEMORY

Besides everything else it does, your brain is a huge hard drive, storing millions and millions of memories. While you can't remember everything you've ever done (what did you have for breakfast on the third of March last year?), your brain is pretty good at remembering the important stuff (your address, or the fact that you hate eating mushrooms). Your memory can sometimes even surprise you—like if you recognize a toy you haven't seen since you were tiny, or if you remember the lyrics to a song you last heard when you were four (like "Humpty Dumpty Sat on a Ball" or "The Eels on the Bus").

SNUGGLE HORSE!

Your memory is brilliant at keeping records of this stuff. What was the part of the brain I told you about earlier that stores all your memories? (Ugh, I can't believe you forgot! I take back everything I said about your memory being brilliant.) Fine, I'll tell you again: the hippocampus.

You know how grown-ups are always walking into a room and saying, "Now, why did I come in here?" or spending an hour looking for their glasses? It's not their fault—as you get older, your hippocampus shrinks, so your memory doesn't work as well. There is also a condition known as dementia that some people get when they're much older that affects their memory. You can lower your risk of dementia by keeping yourself active—not just your body, but also your brain. Doing puzzles is like sending your neurons to the gym. (Except your brain doesn't get all sweaty and collapse in an exhausted heap after twelve minutes like I do when I work out.)

Scientists have calculated that, if the part of your brain that stores memories were a computer, it would have 2 million gigabytes of storage. My phone's only got 128 gigabytes of storage—pathetic. If you printed out the contents of your brain in a book, it would be over ten thousand miles high (and probably wouldn't fit on your bookshelf).

EMOTIONS

Whatever people who make Valentine's cards may tell us, your emotions don't come from your heart, they come from your squishy old brain. When I say emotions, I mean things you feel, like sadness (because you've lost your iPad) or happiness (because you've found your iPad) or anger (because your dog stole your iPad and covered it in drool) or love (because you still love your dog even though she's revolting).

We all get sad or angry from time to time, but some people find themselves sad for long periods and for reasons that are hard to understand. This is called depression, and it's a very common type of mental illness. Any kind of cell in the body can have bad days, and the neurons in the brain are no exception. Just like physical illness, it's no one's fault that it happens. Depression sometimes gets better by chatting about it with a specialist (which is known as talk therapy), sometimes it gets better on its own, and sometimes it requires medicine.

ANXIETY

We all get worried about things. Whether you're stressed about exams or your football team losing or your robot butler malfunctioning again and smashing up the bathroom, it's just what our brains do. In fact, it's one of the main downsides of having a brain.

ANXIETY DISORDER — Some people feel very anxious a lot of the time—so much so that it can interfere with everyday life. This is common, and if you feel like it's something that's happening to you, then you should speak to an adult. It's important not to suffer through it alone.

PANIC ATTACKS — These happen when people have a sudden rush of worry that causes their body to react strongly. They can feel faint, hot, sweaty, sick, short of breath, and shaky, and their heart can feel like it's racing—their fight-or-flight response has kicked in when it shouldn't have. Panic attacks are very frightening, but they're not dangerous, and they won't last long.

PHOBIAS — A phobia is an extreme fear of something that shouldn't be scary, sometimes causing symptoms like panic attacks. People have phobias about a huge number of different things; for example, spiders, going to the dentist, heights, germs, or speaking in public. They often make big changes to their lives to stop any chance of coming across the thing they're scared of. Talk therapy can really help with this. You might never get over the phobia, but you can learn to live without it affecting your life. A fear of spiders is called arachnophobia, a fear of small spaces is called claustrophobia, and a fear of phobias is called phobophobia.

Your brain produces enough energy to light up a light bulb. I don't know how scientists discovered this particular fact, but I'm glad they didn't experiment on me to find it out. . . .

I'm really afraid of heights: I hate walking across bridges, and find it really difficult to go down escalators. You know what? I've never told anyone that before, and now I've just told all of you. It wasn't so bad. Lots of people don't discuss their fears with anyone because they're worried about what others might think or say. But I promise that no one's going to judge you for it; they'll just want to help you to feel better quickly.

STROKE

A stroke means that the brain has had its blood supply interrupted, a bit like what happens to the heart in a heart attack. This could be because a blood vessel in the brain has burst or gotten blocked. The brain needs constant oxygen and fuel to do all its important jobs, so if the blood supply stops for even a moment, then it's a serious emergency. Anyone having a stroke needs an ambulance immediately. Strokes mostly happen to people when they're much older; they occasionally happen to younger people too, but it's very, very rare. They can cause a person's arm or leg to suddenly go weak, or affect their speech or vision.

DRUGS

A drug is anything you put in your body that has an effect on it, so every medicine is technically a drug. But when I say the word, it probably makes you think of illegal drugs. These drugs affect how neurons in the brain send messages to each other, and that changes how you feel or think. There are loads of different types of illegal drugs, including ones that can be smoked, such as cannabis (also

134

known as marijuana, weed, grass, spliffs—it has lots of different names), and pills or powders that can be ingested, such as ecstasy. People take drugs because they like the way they make them feel, but drugs are illegal for a simple reason: they're dangerous. One day in the future, you'll probably meet people who have tried drugs, and they might even offer you some to try yourself. It's okay to say no. Think about what you'll say if someone ever offers you drugs—sometimes it's easier to have somebody else to blame. For example, "I can't—my dad would kill me if he found out," or, "No thanks—I've got to get up really early tomorrow to repair my robot butler."

KAY'S KWESTIONS

WHY DO SOME PEOPLE NEED WHEELCHAIRS?

There are lots of reasons why people get around using wheels instead of feet—for example, they might have had an injury to their spinal cord that means the nerves can't travel down to their feet, so the brain's messages can't get through. Or they might have been born with a condition

I've spoken to the computer shop and they don't have any appointments for a few days. Very annoying. Still, it should be fixed uite soon.

that affects their muscles (such as muscular dystrophy) or their nerves (such as cerebral palsy). They can go to school like everybody else, and when they're older they can go to work and drive cars—do everything, really!

HOW MUCH SLEEP DO I NEED?

Kids generally need between eight and ten hours of sleep every night, but everyone is different. Thomas Edison, who invented microphones, light bulbs, and movie cameras, only slept for four hours a night—maybe he was too busy inventing stuff to have any time for napping.

If you need inspiration to get more zzzzs, super-mega-genius Albert Einstein slept for ten hours a night.

WHAT CAUSES BRAIN FREEZE?

Sometimes when you eat ice cream or drink a really cold drink, you get "brain freeze"—a short, sharp, horrible headache that can really spoil your chocolate chip cookie dough raspberry ripple supreme with multicolored sprinkles and pieces of walnut. (Please check that you're actually eating pieces of walnut and not pieces of cerebellum.) You'll be relieved to hear that it's not actually your brain freezing. It's because your nerves have gotten mixed up and sent pain signals to your brain by accident, when they were sensing cold temperatures. Stupid nerves.

WHY DO I GET PINS AND NEEDLES?

Pins and needles is the name for a feeling like someone is jabbing your skin with pins and needles. One cause for this is that someone is actually jabbing your skin with pins and needles. More commonly, it happens when you sit in the same position for too long or lean on your arm for ages. If you put pressure on a nerve, it blocks the pathway between your brain and your foot or arm— you've essentially broken the Wi-Fi. Once you change position and the nerve can work again, it goes a bit haywire, causing pins and needles. Or paresthesia, if you want to use its doctory name.

TRUE OR POO?

GENIUSES HAVE MASSIVE BRAINS.

POO You might think that having a brain the size of a bungalow would mean acing all your exams, but it doesn't actually work like that. The brain of smarty-pants Albert Einstein—one of the smartest people who ever lived—was weighed after he died, and it was actually smaller than average. (Right after he died, someone stole his brain—maybe they thought it would help them cheat at school?—and it wasn't found until years later.) One of the main things that affects how smart you are is how smart your parents are—which is bad news for me, because I once watched my dad spend over an hour trying to change the time on the microwave.

YOU CAN PLAY A MUSICAL INSTRUMENT WHILE SOMEONE IS OPERATING ON YOUR BRAIN.

TRUE You might think this is strange, but because the brain itself doesn't feel any pain, you can be awake during brain surgery. Recently, a patient played the violin the entire time she was having her operation. I hope she wasn't terrible at the violin, or it must have been very distracting for her doctors. *Screech! Screech! Screech!*

YOU ONLY USE TEN PERCENT
OF YOUR BRAIN.

POO This is a very common myth, and I
don't really know why people think this. There
aren't any spare parts of your brain that don't get
used—every little wrinkle of squishy gray stuff has a job
to do.

YOUR BRAIN CAN REPAIR ITSELF LIKE SKIN.

POO Unfortunately, your brain can't repair itself very
well. Unlike your skin, which is always making new
cells, your brain is quite happy with the neurons it
already has, so it doesn't create any extra. That means
you need to look after the ones you have very carefully,
and it's why you always need to wear a helmet on your
bike even though it messes up your hair.

THAT ONE LOOKS LIKE ME,
THAT ONE LOOKS LIKE ME,
THAT ONE LOOKS LIKE ME . . .

CHAPTER 6
HAIR AND NAILS

WE LAVISH a lot of attention on our hair, don't we? We wash it all the time, we buy expensive products to make it look and smell great, and every couple of months we toddle off to the hairdresser to keep it stylish. Our kidneys must be so jealous—when was the last time you bought some kidney gel or went to the kidneydresser? Of course, the thing about hair is that it's pretty unmissable—it's one of the first things people notice about you, unless you're wearing a massive hat or travel everywhere on the back of a zebra. But there's a lot more to hair than that untamed fluff on the top of your head—you have hair almost everywhere, and it has some pretty important jobs to do.

WHAT IS HAIR?

There are five million hairs on your body, which is the same as the number of people in Ireland. There you go—you've learned two facts at once. No extra charge. Only a tiny portion of your hairs are on your head (about two percent), but luckily the ones on the rest of your body aren't quite as noticeable—otherwise you'd look like my dog, and you'd spend a fortune in shampoo.

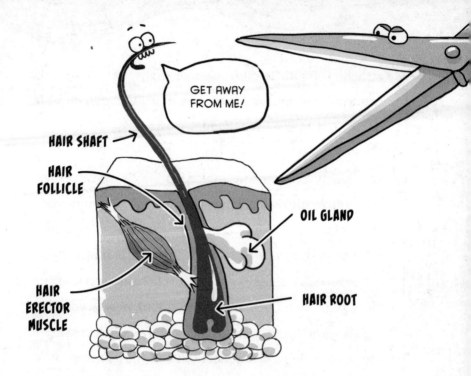

Hair grows out of little tubes buried in our skin, which are called follicles. Each hair grows from a root at the bottom and up through the skin, and it's made from a substance called keratin. Keratin is extremely strong, and it's what horses' hooves and rhinos' horns are made of. In fact, the hair on your head is so strong that it could lift an elephant without snapping. (Please don't try to lift an elephant with your hair. Your hair might be tough enough, but your scalp isn't. Plus, you'd need to hire a crane to dangle from, and the elephant probably wouldn't be thrilled about any of this.) Every hair follicle is attached to a little oil dispenser that makes your hair beautiful and glossy (if you live in a TV show) or a bit greasy (if you live in real life).

Your hair color is genetic, which means it's passed down through families, so you know where to send your complaint if you don't like it. If your hair isn't the same color as one of your biological parents, then see if you can look back through some family photo albums (they're like a printed-out version of Instagram). Maybe you had a great-great-grandparent with the same hair color as you—it can skip a few generations! (If you look at photos that are extremely old, then they'll be in black-and-white, so that won't help you much.) Just like your skin, the color of your hair is determined by melanin. More melanin means darker hair. Red hair is the rarest of all the hair colors—only one in 50 people in the world has it. (Technically, purple-and-silver stripes is actually the rarest hair color, but I was talking about colors that don't come out of a spray can.) The amount of melanin in your hair can increase until you're ten, so it's possible for your hair to get darker—just in case you've ever looked at photos of yourself from when you were little and wondered why you were wearing a wig.

So, what's the point of all this hair, other than decoration? Well, as you might remember from the chapter on the skin, your body hair has an ingenious way of warming you up—by standing on end using a minuscule muscle and trapping a layer of air. (If you can't remember, please reread the chapter about the brain because maybe your brain has fallen out.) Then, when it's hot, the hair on your head reflects the sun's rays like a fuzzy parasol so you don't overheat—clever, huh?

HAIR IN DIFFERENT WEATHER:

OTHER TYPES OF HAIR

EYEBROWS

Forgot your hat? Relax—your eyebrows have got you covered, literally. They provide a handy visor to keep the sun out of your eyes, as well as pushing sweat and rain out of the way so your eyes can do important things like reading this book. Did you know that you actually have twelve separate noses? Okay, fine—that's not true. But reading it might have made your eyebrows shoot up— that's what we do when we're surprised. Humans have been doing this since before language was invented, and we still haven't shaken the habit after all these years.

EYELASHES

Eyelashes aren't just there to snazz up your eyelids. Think about what happens when it's windy and there's dust flying around—your eyes narrow so that your lovely lashes can bat away any dirt heading your way. They're also the closest thing you have to whiskers—feeling for anything that might get in your eye, then telling your eyes to slam shut if there's danger nearby. That's what blinking is. Your eyelashes also have a side gig as a disgusting zoo. Yep, living in your lashes are hundreds of miniature monsters called **DEMODEX**. They feed on dead skin and oil from your face and only come out at night because they don't like being seen. (You wouldn't like being seen either if you looked like one of them.) There's no need to worry, though—everyone has them, they're so small you can only see them with a microscope, and most importantly, they don't chew your face off while you're asleep. Promise.

PUBIC HAIR

You get a lot of extra bonus hair around puberty, and it's a sign that you're growing up. It appears under your arms and between your legs, but we don't exactly know why your body puts it there. One theory is that it's good at keeping sweat away from your skin so it doesn't stink too much. Other people think that it's there as some kind of weird in-built Vaseline, to stop your skin from rubbing together and getting sore. Other than that—no idea, sorry. You're on your own. If you figure out what it's for, let me know, and I'll put it in the next edition of this book. (I'll probably pretend it was my idea, though.)

NOSE HAIR

See that carpet of hair sprouting out of your uncle's nostrils? Nose hair has a job (other than putting you off your dinner): it stops dust and pollen and massive bumblebees from going up your nose and into your lungs.

FACIAL HAIR

When puberty comes around, boys sprout hair on their faces because they have a high level of testosterone. Testosterone is a hormone, which means it's part of the body's messaging system. Girls have the same number of hair follicles, but have lower testosterone levels, so there's usually much less hair growth. Boys get facial hair from about the age of eleven, but it'll be scraggly bits to start with, only becoming beardier in their twenties. I used to have a beard until I found out a couple of years ago that nearly half of all beards contain tiny amounts of poop . . . and then I got my robot butler to shave it off.

Your hair grows faster in the summer than in the winter—like a horrible, hairy plant. On average, every year it grows by about the length of your hand. Disappointingly, if you never cut your hair, it won't just grow forever until you look like a human mop. Each hair can only keep growing for a few years, before it falls out and clogs up your plug hole. (When a hair falls out at your age, it just gets replaced with another one—you won't be as bald as an egg any time soon.) If your hair never fell out and just kept growing, in a lifetime it would grow to be seven times as tall as you.

BAD HAIR DAYS

HEAD LICE

Chances are you've already spent a bit of quality time with head lice. They're cute little things, really. If you ignore the fact that they've got sharp claws that dig into your scalp and they drink your blood. Surprisingly, this doesn't hurt, because they're only the size of a grain of sand, but it can make your head feel pretty itchy. The lice themselves aren't very easy to see, but you might spot the little white eggs they hatch out of, known as nits. Because they enjoy spending time with their friends, you don't just get one head louse—there will probably be more like fifty of them. (And it could be as many as a thousand. *Aaaagh!*)

Head lice don't care how dirty or clean your hair is, so you haven't done anything that's caused them to appear. That said, these are guests you didn't invite to your party, so it's quite reasonable to want them to leave. Unfortunately, asking them politely doesn't seem to work, so you'll need to have your hair brushed with a special comb while it's still wet.

This generally sorts things out, but if the lice can't bear to leave your delicious scalp, you might need to get a lotion or potion from the pharmacy. I've got some really terrible news about head lice, though. Are you ready for this? You still have to go to school if you have them. I'm so sorry.

GRAY HAIR

Unlike you or me, who will have to work until we're in our sixties, the melanin in your hair can choose to retire any time. It might happen before you're twenty, or it might wait until you're seventy, or it might never happen. If melanin hangs up its colored coat, your hair will go gray or white. You might hear grown-ups moaning that you're causing them so much stress it's turning their hair gray. Even though it sounds bananas, it's actually a real thing. Stress can make your body release certain hormones, and one of them can lower your melanin supplies. It doesn't turn hair gray overnight, though, so hopefully by the time this happens it'll be too late to prove it was anything to do with you drawing all over the wallpaper or covering the kitchen with mayonnaise.

DANDRUFF

No, it's not snowing in small patches on your shoulders—that's dandruff, or seborrheic dermatitis, to use Mr. Druff's proper name. Dandruff means the scalp gets itchy, and little bits of skin float off. It often shows its flaky head at puberty because the scalp gets more oily around then, but the good news is it usually goes away after using a special shampoo.

HAIR LOSS

You might have noticed that some older men, like dads, grandads, teachers, and Professor X, may not have as much hair as they did when they were younger. This is called male pattern baldness, and it's the most common cause of hair loss—it happens to most men as they get older, like moaning about the traffic and wearing cardigans.

WHERE DID EVERYONE GO?

Sometimes it also happens to women, and sometimes hair falls out for other reasons, like stress, illness, or powerful medicines such as cancer treatment—which might make the hair grow back different from how it was before. And sometimes hair can fall out in patches because your body's natural defense mechanisms attack the hair follicles by accident. This is called **ALOPECIA**. There are many types and it can happen at any age to men and women. Sometimes the hair grows back and sometimes it doesn't—but with or without hair, you're always still you.

Some men get very stressed about how hair loss makes them look, so they take medicine to try to stop any more from falling out, or even have operations or hair transplants from other parts of their body. This doesn't always work, but it works a lot better than what the ancient Greeks did. They thought the answer was smearing their heads with pigeon poop.

NAILS

Who would choose to be a nail? You might get lucky and be pampered and groomed and painted in beautiful colors and patterns. More likely you'll end up gunked with dirt and getting bitten all day. But there's more to nails than decoration/lovely snacks (delete according to how revolting you are). They have a pretty simple job: to protect the ends of your fingers and toes and stop them from getting injured. They can do this because they're made of keratin, which you'll remember is very strong stuff. Your nails are tougher than your hair because the keratin is packed in a lot tighter. Nails are so strong that you can hammer them into the wall to hold up pictures. No, hang on, that's a different type of nail.

Your nails also have side jobs, like the way some people work in offices during the day and drive taxis in the evening, or the way your math teacher is also a secret burglar at night.

The record for the longest fingernails was held by a woman named Lee Redmond. Added together, her nails were over 26 feet long, which is about half as long as a lane at a bowling alley. I hope she didn't have to do much typing.

Your nails help you grip things, peel things, and climb things, and they tell your brain how hard your finger's pressing down on something. Handy, right? Handy . . . like on a hand? Oh, for goodness' sake—I give up.

Nails grow from the nail root, which is under the cuticle (that curved bit of skin you can see at the base of your nails). The cuticle is a bit like a draft insulator under a door, and it stops germs from slipping in. Nails grow very slowly—less than a millimeter a week—so if you have an accident and your fingernail comes off, it might take a good few months to grow a whole new one.

Scientists have a name for biting your nails: **onychophagia**. You also have a word for it: lunch.

KAY'S KWESTIONS

WHY DOESN'T IT HURT WHEN YOU CUT YOUR HAIR AND NAILS?

Imagine if it did! Hairdressers would go out of business and nail clippers would be banned by the police as deadly weapons. The simple answer is that your hair and nails are dead cells with no nerve endings, and if there are no nerves somewhere, you can't feel any pain. The nail bed underneath your nails is alive, though, which is why it hurts so much if you accidentally cut a nail too short.

My laptop's going into the shop tomorrow. Fingers crossed they can fix the letter Q.

WHY IS SOME PEOPLE'S HAIR STRAIGHT AND OTHER PEOPLE'S HAIR CURLY?

It's all about the follicles—those tiny tubes your hair grows out of. If you're born with follicles that are perfectly circular tubes, then your hair will grow straight. The more oval (or squished) the tube that the hair comes out of, the curlier your hair will be. Like a lot of things about hair, this is all genetic. If you've got curly hair, then your biological parents probably do too. (Either that or they use straighteners . . .)

WILL YOU CATCH A COLD IF YOU GO OUTSIDE WITH WET HAIR?

When I was a child I got told all the time that going out with wet hair would make me catch a cold. It wasn't until I went to medical school that I found out this was total nonsense. Why do grown-ups tell us this stuff? Absolute idiots.

TRUE OR POO?

YOU HAVE HAIR ON EVERY PART OF YOUR BODY.

POO Most parts, but not *quite* everywhere. You'll never have any reason to shave the palms of your hands, the soles of your feet, your nipples, or your lips.

YOUR FINGERNAILS KEEP GROWING AFTER YOU DIE.

POO You might have heard this before, because people used to think it was true. What actually happens after death is that the skin around the base of the fingernails pulls back a bit, making it look like the nails have grown. Ugh.

FINGERNAILS GROW FASTER THAN TOENAILS.

TRUE Your fingernails grow two or three times as fast as your toenails, which is good because it's much harder to bite your toenails down to size. (Don't pretend you haven't tried.) Your fingernails grow faster on the hand you use the most, and the longer the finger, the faster the nail grows.

EYES

I BELIEVE IT WAS William Shakespeare who once wrote, "The eyes are the windows to your soul." Well, he must have been a total idiot, because they're nothing like windows. They're actually more like cameras—the most advanced cameras in the world, in fact. They observe millions of things every second, then send all that information to your brain at super-speed to make sense of what you've seen. The only problem with these particular cameras is you can't put filters on them to improve your family's terrible haircuts.

The part of your eye you can see in the mirror is only about a sixth of your eyeball. The rest of it is safely nestled away in protective circles of bone in the skull, known as your eye sockets. Your eyes also get protected on the outside by your eyelids. Honestly, they're treated like royalty. But for those of us lucky enough to have the power of sight, it's important to do what we can to keep it.

An ostrich's eye is bigger than its brain. (I won't make any rude comments about the size of your brain. But I thought about it.)

So let's take a peek inside your peepers.

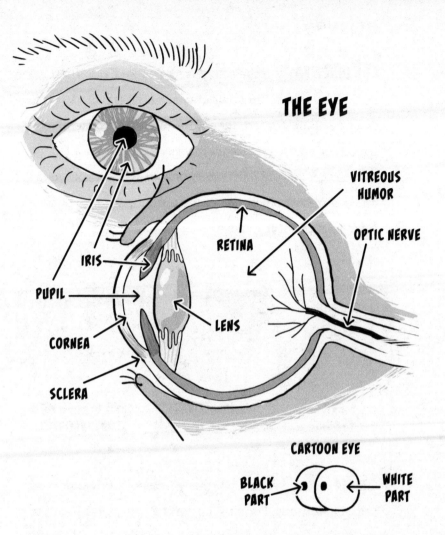

THE EYE

VITREOUS HUMOR

OPTIC NERVE

RETINA

IRIS

PUPIL

LENS

CORNEA

SCLERA

CARTOON EYE

BLACK PART → ← **WHITE PART**

SCLERA — Just like the white part is the boring part when you're eating an egg, the white of your eye isn't that interesting either. Your sclera is like a coating of white paint that's there to protect your eyessssssssssssss. Sorry, I got so bored by the sclera that I just fell asleep on my keyboard.

CONJUNCTIVA — If the sclera is like white paint, then the conjunctiva is a thin layer of varnish on top of it. If this layer goes pink or red, then it means either you're an evil cyborg or you've got conjunctivitis, which is an infection that can make your eye watery or sore. It often goes away on its own but sometimes needs eye drops. I have no idea what to suggest if you're an evil cyborg.

EVIL
CYBORG

CONJUNCTIVITIS

EVIL CYBORG WITH
CONJUNCTIVITIS

CORNEA — I spy with my little eye, something beginning with C. Actually, I don't. The cornea is rather difficult to spot, because it's totally see-through. It has to be, because . . . well, it's the bit you see through (otherwise it would be like wearing a pair of smeary glasses all the time). It's also a very fast healer—if the cornea gets scratched, it can mend itself in a couple of days. The lazy old skin could learn a lesson or two from the cornea.

VITREOUS HUMOR — Where would we be without humor? Well, if you're talking about the vitreous humor in your eye, it

Some people have two different-colored eyes—this is very rare and has a special medical name (I mean, what doesn't): **heterochromia**.

would mean you wouldn't be able to see. It's the fluid inside your eyeball that stops it from looking like a deflated balloon.

IRIS — The iris is the colored part of the eye. Once again, it's melanin that decides the color: more melanin means darker eyes. The most common eye color is . . . drumroll, please . . . brown, which about eight out of ten people have. The rarest eye color is bright yellow with pink polka dots and a diagonal gold stripe, which no one has.

PUPIL — Your pupils don't really exist, sorry. I know, I know—you've got black dots in the middle of your eyes, but they're actually just holes in your iris rather than an actual *thing*. The iris changes the size of this hole to decide how much light to let in. If it's bright, the pupils shrink down until they're tiny. If it's dark, they open up wide to allow as much light in as possible—your eyes literally open the blinds to make it brighter in there.

LENS — This is the name for a group of people called Len. It's also the name for a little magnifying glass that sits behind the iris. You probably know the word

SAY CHEESE!

"lens" from cameras, and the ones in your eyes do exactly the same thing: they focus the image that comes in and project it to the back of the eye (a bit like how a projector shines a film onto the screen at the movie theater). Our lenses change shape to help the eye focus—they get fatter to look at something close by (like your phone), and get thinner if you're staring at something far away (like a spaceship).

RETINA — The retina is made up of millions and millions of receptors that tell the brain what your eyes are looking at. There are two different types of receptors: rods and cones. The cones see things in color, and the rods see things in black-and-white, like an old TV. The rods and cones send the signals they pick up brainward using a nerve called the optic nerve. Then finally your brain gets on with the important business of deciding if you're looking at a trash bag, a radiator, or a model of the Eiffel Tower made out of cucumbers.

Some people sleep with their eyes open—this is called **nocturnal lagophthalmos**. It's not very common, but it's something to chat to a doctor about because it can make your eyes sore. Also, it's pretty freaky for your friends at sleepovers.

If you're wondering why owls always move their heads about, it's because their eyes are locked in position, so it's the only way they're able to look left or right. We're not like owls, because our eyes move around using six muscles that yank them in all different directions. And also we don't eat mice. Usually, both eyes look in the same direction as each other; when they point in slightly different directions it's known as strabismus. This is very common, but strabismus can often be corrected—by wearing glasses, doing eye exercises, or having an operation. Sometimes strabismus doesn't go away, though, and it's just part of what makes someone unique!

OTHER FUNCTIONS OF THE EYE

So, we've established that your eyes are good at seeing, but what else do they get up to? Well, quite a lot, as it turns out—for example, blinking, crying, and shooting lasers.

BLINKING

Your eyelids aren't just shutters that come down at night—they're hard at work all through the day too. When you blink, it's like a watering system that coats your eyes with a thin layer of liquid. And, unlike when you promised to water your grandparents' plants when they were away, your eyelids never accidentally forget.

In fact, they do it nearly twenty thousand times a day. Blinking can also give your eyes a bit of shade if there's a sudden bright light, and it gets rid of any dirt that accidentally finds its way in there. Eyelids are your body's very own flesh-colored windshield wipers.

CRYING

You'd probably panic if water started pouring out of your ears or your fingernails (and I wouldn't blame you), but somehow we don't think it's weird that water comes out of our eyes. Tears aren't just there to show the world that we're sad or laughing our heads off, they're also part of your eyes' natural defenses, washing out anything nasty that's got in there. That's why your eyes water if you have allergies—your tears are trying to rinse the pollen out. Tears come from glands in the top corner of your eye sockets, and besides streaming down your face, they also drain into the nose—that's why crying sometimes gives you a runny nose.

E E
T Z
LPED
PECFDZM
HENRYPAKERISAREALLYCOOLGUY

SHOOTING LASERS

My mistake. I think that's just something I've seen in movies.

GLASSES

Your eyes are complex bits of equipment, so it's only natural that they'll occasionally need a bit of help to get everything right. In fact, most of us will need to wear glasses at some point. Remember how the lens gets fatter and thinner to focus the things you see onto your retina? Well, sometimes your lenses aren't so great at doing this, so what you see looks blurry. It's very common to need glasses as you get older. Just like older people's skin gets a bit saggier until it just hangs there like laundry, so do the lenses in their eyes.

I'm sure you've woken up before with weird, sticky gunk in your eyes—sometimes it's slimy, sometimes it's dried out, and sometimes it sticks your eyelids together. It's a mixture of mucus, dust, and skin cells (in case you wanted to know the recipe).

When you're awake your eyes just blink it all away, but when it's night and your eyelids are off duty it builds up like a disgusting glue for you to deal with in the morning.

Some people are farsighted, which means that they see things okay if they're far away, but everything looks blurry up close. That's why people often hold their phone at arm's length so they can read messages. Other people have the opposite problem, and are nearsighted: they can see things close by, but can't see things that are farther away quite as well. Glasses are a second lens that you wear on the outside of your eyes to focus everything correctly onto your retina.

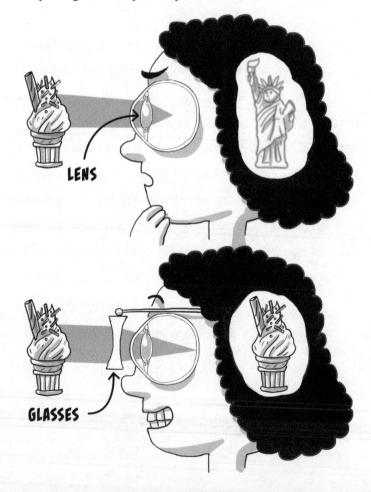

LENS

GLASSES

This is good news because glasses are cool. Some adults can have laser eye surgery, which disappointingly still doesn't mean you can shoot lasers from your eyes—instead, a doctor shoots a laser *into* them, which makes tiny adjustments to the lenses so they can focus correctly.

SIGHT LOSS

Some people have more serious issues with their eyes that they're either born with or develop over time. This might mean they permanently lose their sight, either partially (so they still have limited vision) or completely (so they can't see at all). Sometimes the issue affects both eyes, and sometimes it affects one eye so that the other has to work a bit harder. There are lots of different reasons why someone can't see well—their eyes might not have developed properly, or they might have been affected by conditions such as infections, diabetes, or certain types of cancer. Some people also lose their vision because they damage their eyes in accidents—this is why it's extremely important never to poke someone in the eye, even lightly or as a joke.

People with sight loss lead fun and interesting lives, have jobs, and do practically everything that people with regular vision do. Technology means that computers can read out what's on a screen or in a book. Before this, Braille was the most common way for blind people to read—it's a kind of writing where the words are made up of little bumps on the page that you read by running your fingers across them. Some people with sight loss use a white cane (like a stick) when they walk, which they tap on the ground or sweep from side to side in front of them to check if there are any obstacles ahead. Other people might walk arm in arm with a helper, and some might have a guide dog, who makes sure they can get around safely. Guide dogs are trained from when they're tiny puppies, and they're extremely clever and well behaved. (Pippin would be the most disastrous guide dog ever—always chasing after birds and sniffing poop.) If you see a guide dog, you must never pet them without asking their human first—guide dogs are busy doing their job, and you shouldn't interrupt someone who's at work, no matter how many legs they've got or how cute they are!

EARS

Our poor ears. We jab sharp bits of metal through them and call them earrings, we shove our fingers inside them to dig around for wax, and we force them to listen to terrible music. But when was the last time you thought about what's going on inside those flappy friends at the sides of your head?

Your ears' main job is to collect the sounds being made all around you, then whizz them off to your brain, which works out whether the noise is a truck reversing, someone playing the guitar, or your dog farting.

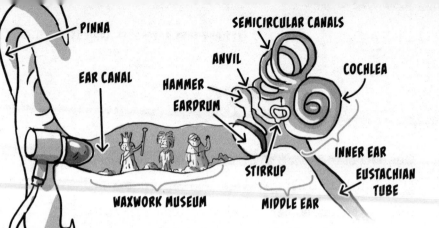

PINNA — Your ears are like icebergs. What? No, they're not freezing cold. No, they're not covered in penguins. Okay, fine—they're not *exactly* like icebergs. I just meant that a lot of them is hidden away, out of sight. Your pinna is the part you *can* see on the outside and it's made of cartilage, which means it's tough but bendy. It's shaped like that so it can trap sounds and funnel them inside your head like a satellite dish.

EAR CANAL — The canals in Venice are one of the wonders of the modern world—beautiful, tranquil, and romantic. The canals in your ears are little tubes that fill up with wax—not quite as good for sailing a gondola in, and significantly less romantic. They're the holes that doctors look in if you're feeling unwell, and they're where

you stick your fingers if you don't want to hear what your teacher is saying.

EARDRUM — Also known as the tympanic membrane (if you want to be fancy about it), this is a very thin sheet of tissue right inside your ear canal, stretched tight across, like an actual drumskin. Instead of getting hit with drumsticks, though, the eardrum moves when it's hit by sound waves.

MIDDLE EAR — Can you guess where in the ear you find the middle ear? That's right—in the middle. You win thirty-six million dollars. The middle ear is a space on the other side of your eardrum with three tiny bones in it called the malleus, the incus, and the stapes, or the hammer, the anvil, and the stirrup. (Not sure why the naming committee gave them all two names each. Maybe Clive was bored.) These bite-sized bones work in a chain to transmit vibrations that the sound waves make into the inner ear. Oh, sorry—I lied about the thirty-six million dollars. I do hope you haven't already spent it.

INNER EAR — Your inner ear is home to your cochlea, which is a tiny snail-shaped thing nestled deep inside

your head. The cochlea has the important job of turning all the vibrations into nerve signals that can be sent to your brain, and it does this using thousands and thousands of tiny little hairs.

While there are many issues with your ears that you can't control (and I don't just mean their size), there are a few things you can do to try to keep them healthy. Firstly, don't stick things in them. I'm serious. Your fingers, cotton swabs, pencils, other people's fingers, anything. Even if you have a really annoying bit of wax that you're dying to set free. You might actually push the earwax deeper inside, which could damage the eardrum. And this may sound like I'm asking you to stop breathing or never pet a dog again, but here goes: turn the volume down on your headphones, the TV, and your games, or you can end up really damaging your hearing. No, your parents didn't pay me to write that—it's true. The problem with hearing damage is that it can build up slowly over time, so you don't notice it right away, and when you finally do, it can be too late.

HOW DOES SHE DO IT?

BALANCE

Your inner ear has a surprising second job: it's a backup dancer in the Broadway production of the musical *Cats*. No, that doesn't sound right. It's in charge of making you stand up straight. Next to the cochlea are three little curved tubes full of fluid called the semicircular canals, which tell the brain if your head is moving. Ever wondered why you feel dizzy when you've just staggered off a massive roller coaster? It's because the fluid in the semicircular canals is still moving, so your brain thinks you're spinning around. But because your eyes tell your brain that you're just standing there, it gets confused, and suddenly . . . whoa, everything goes a bit weird. This is also what makes you feel seasick—your inner ear tells your brain that you're moving, your eyes look around the boat and say everything's staying still, and all of a sudden your body gets in a muddle and that cheeseburger you had for lunch makes an unexpected comeback all over the floor.

EARWAX

There's lots of stuff in your ears that you've probably never seen. (I hope you've never seen your cochlea or the bones of your middle ear, for example—they're very much designed to stay inside your body.) But I'm sure you're well acquainted with that weird, slimy, yellowy-brown gunk that you might know as earwax (and doctors know as cerumen). Earwax is one of your body's defenses, trapping dirt in its sticky icky grasp to stop it getting into your ear's inner machinery and causing infections. It also protects the skin of your ear canal by keeping it nicely moisturized.

Unlike your teeth and your bedroom, your ears are self-cleaning, and the earwax will find its way out of your ear when it's finished vacuuming up dirt, usually falling out when you're asleep. Sometimes your ears can get a bit blocked with earwax, though, causing pain or making it harder to hear things. As I hope you'll remember from *literally seconds ago,* you must never put anything in your ears, and that includes cotton swabs. If your ear canals are wax central, then it's possible to melt the wax so it all comes out. Luckily, no one needs to shove a lit match

SOME OF US ARE TRYING TO SLEEP!

in there—there are drops that your nearest friendly grown-up can get from the pharmacy. If that doesn't work, then it's off to the doctor, who might need to suck it out with a mini vacuum.

EAR INFECTIONS

Pain in your ear? Check. Temperature? Check. Gross fluid coming out? Check. Sounds like an ear infection— that means there's some pus in there trying to escape. Your middle ear has a fire exit, called the **EUSTACHIAN TUBE** (not to be confused with Euston Station tube, which is a place in London), that can drain fluid into the throat—please try not to think about how disgusting this is. Your Eustachian tube can sometimes get blocked, making it all very uncomfortable in there. Your doctor will look inside your ears using a light. Then they might decide it will settle down on its own or they might give you some medicine to help it clear up.

Animals who need to hear extremely well have huge ears (okay, pinnas) to amplify the sound so they can even hear an ant farting. Elephants don't need their massive ears for hearing, though—heat escapes from their ears, which helps them cool down in the hot sun. Asian elephants live in cooler climates than African elephants, so they have smaller ears.

The little hairs inside your cochlea really don't like loud noises. If you go somewhere loud they flatten down, which is why your hearing might not be as good for a few hours afterward. If you know you're going to go somewhere loud, then it's sensible to wear earplugs, because too much loud noise can cause permanent damage. Also, earplugs mean you don't need to listen to what any grown-ups are saying to you.

The eardrum is like any other kind of drum—if you hit it too hard, it can burst. If you have a severe ear infection and don't get it treated, then the build-up of pus (sorry if you're eating) can make it pop. Another way that eardrums burst is by getting poked by something like a cotton swab. (I told you they were bad. . . .) Really loud noises, such as explosions, can burst eardrums too, and it can also happen by slapping someone's ears (not that you would ever do something horrible like that). Finally, dramatic changes in air pressure can burst eardrums—this sometimes happens to scuba divers. Burst eardrums generally heal on their own, but occasionally they need surgery, and there's a small chance your hearing will never fully recover. What I'm saying is, try not to get a hole there in the first place!

HEARING LOSS

Over six million people in the US are deaf or have some difficulty hearing. Some people are born with a form of hearing loss; for others it happens in childhood or later in life. There are lots of reasons this can happen. For example, smoking makes it more likely you'll develop hearing loss when you're older. Yet another reason (to add to the zillion others) why you shouldn't smoke.

Some deaf people and people with hearing loss lip-read (that's exactly what you'd think it is—understanding what someone is saying by watching their lips move), and others use sign language, which means moving their hands and face to communicate. Watching TV isn't a problem either— some programs have subtitles, and others have a tiny man or woman in the corner translating everything into sign language.

American Sign Language is totally different from British Sign Language—if you know American Sign Language, then the British kind is literally a foreign language. In fact, American Sign Language is much closer to French Sign Language than it is to British.

119

I mean, they're usually average-sized people, but they've been shrunk down. I mean, they haven't literally been shrunk down—the picture of them has been.

Some people with hearing loss wear hearing aids, which are tiny little speakers that amplify sound. There are many different kinds of hearing aids. Some hearing aids sit behind the ear, and other smaller ones go right inside it. I bet you've spoken to people with hearing aids before and not even realized it.

You might have heard about someone going from not hearing anything their entire life to suddenly being able to hear after receiving a cochlear implant. This is a type of hearing aid that is placed in the cochlea during an operation, which sends electrical signals directly to the brain. It's totally amazing technology—plus, because you've got some electronics implanted inside you, I think it means you're technically a cyborg, which is pretty cool.

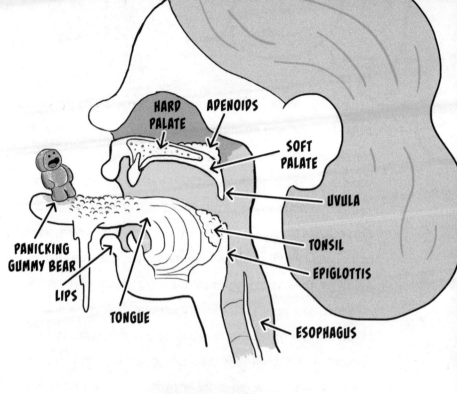

MOUTH

There's a lot going on in that blabbering old mouth of yours, so take a seat and I'll show you around.

TONSILS — You might already know your tonsils from their starring role in that old classic, tonsillitis. But there's more to tonsils than getting all inflamed and making you feel like you've been gargling gravel. They're your mouth's bodyguards—hanging around at the back of your throat and battling any germs that are planning on getting in. Tonsils are great friends with the adenoids, which do similar work higher up in your throat, behind your nose. But just like even doctors get sick sometimes, your tonsils can become infected themselves—this is called tonsillitis. They become red and swollen, even covered in pus, and this can cause swelling in your neck too. Sometimes tonsillitis will get better on its own, and sometimes you'll need to take medicine. If it's painful to swallow, then your doctor might recommend you eat ice cream to soothe it. (You didn't read that wrong—a doctor might literally insist that you eat ice cream.) If your tonsils are getting infected very regularly, or if they've gotten so big that it affects your breathing, then it might be necessary to have an operation to take them out—this is called a tonsillectomy. (*Ectomy* at the end of a word means removing that part of the body. Like an appendectomy or a buttectomy.)

UVULA — Ever wondered if that dangly thing at the back of your mouth has a name? Well, this is your lucky day— it's called the uvula. It's there for the extremely important function of making a growling sound when you're doing an impression of a lion. Oh, and it also helps make saliva.

PALATE — The roof of your mouth is known as your palate. It's divided into a hard bit at the front, called the hard palate, and a soft bit at the back, called the soft palate. Honestly, no imagination whatsoever—I think I'm going to write a letter of complaint to Clive. The soft palate closes off your nostrils when you eat, and stops you from getting a nose full of nachos, which would be rather unpleasant (but might make your boogers taste more interesting).

LIPS — It's good you've got lips, because otherwise your mouth wouldn't close properly and it would be disgusting to watch anyone eat. Also, you couldn't speak properly, and kissing would involve people smashing their teeth together.

TONGUE — I don't know about you, but I'm a big fan of things like talking and eating, so I'd be really annoyed if my tongue fell out, because I wouldn't be able to do either of those. The tongue is covered with thousands of tiny bumps, known as taste buds, which team up with the sensors in your nose to let your brain know whether you're eating a delicious noodle or a disgusting poodle. Your tongue also helps you move food around your mouth, then chuck it back down your throat like a dump truck.

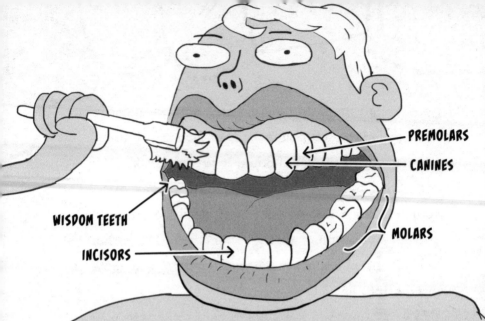

PREMOLARS

CANINES

WISDOM TEETH

MOLARS

INCISORS

TEETH

Now that you can taste food, it's time to chew it. First to arrive are your baby teeth, or milk teeth, or primary teeth if we're going to be all scientific about it. They usually start to appear after a few months, and you end up with twenty of them. One by one, the adult (or permanent) teeth nudge these out the way and they fall out. Your adult teeth usually start to appear around the age of five or six, so calling them "adult" teeth is pushing it slightly. Put your baby teeth under your pillow and . . . *cha-ching!* It's weird how you get money for your old teeth but not for your fingernails or scabs. Imagine if there were a scab fairy. Actually, stop imagining that, it's making me feel ill.

Dentists call it "eruption" when your adult teeth come through, which sounds much more dramatic than it actually is. Still, I guess if your job is looking into people's mouths all day long then you have to find excitement where you can. Most of your teeth are actually under the surface—the lower part of your tooth is called the root, because it buries deep in your jawbone like the roots of a plant.

You have 32 adult teeth:

8 INCISORS — These are the sharp teeth at the front of your mouth. To "incise" means to cut, and that's exactly what they're there for—your own personal set of cutlery.

4 CANINES — Yes, canine, like a dog. They're the next teeth along from your incisors, and they're for tearing into food, like when Pippin destroys my brand-new pair of sneakers for no reason whatsoever.

8 PREMOLARS — These are for crushing up food, like the back of a garbage truck.

8 MOLARS — These have flat tops to grind food up even smaller, like a pepper mill. It's really important that your food gets chewed properly. Otherwise you can upset your intestines (and you don't want to upset them, I promise you).

Your lips are red or pink because their skin is much thinner than the skin on the rest of your body, so you can see the blood vessels underneath!

4 WISDOM TEETH — These are at the very back of your mouth, and they keep hitting the snooze button until you're eighteen or older. Wisdom teeth sometimes come out wonky and need to be removed. (By a dentist, I mean—you don't have to do it yourself.) They're called wisdom teeth because you're *apparently* wiser when you get them than when your other teeth appeared, which makes me think Clive is very biased against children. Right, that's two letters of complaint now.

Bones and teeth might be the same color, but your teeth aren't actually made out of bone. We know this because your teeth can't fix themselves like bones can. Bad news for you, good news for dentists. Once you've broken a tooth, it's broken for good—or until the next set comes along, if you still have your baby teeth.

On the outside, your teeth are made of a thing called **ENAMEL** — this is the hardest substance in the body. It can put up with an awful lot, but it does have its limits— sugary and acidic food can be very damaging, as is not brushing your teeth regularly. That's why it's so important to brush your teeth at least twice a minute. No, sorry—twice a day. Phew. If the enamel

You are born with all the teeth you'll ever have—the adult teeth just sit underneath the milk teeth, like a double-decker bus.

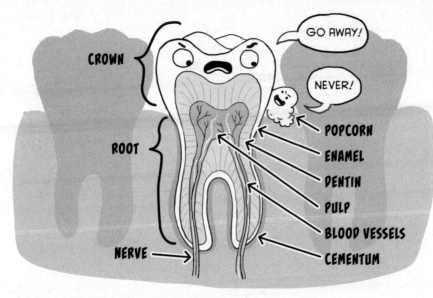

wears away, it exposes the inner workings of your teeth. This can give you a terrible toothache, and you might even need fillings, which are bits of plastic or metal to fill in the gaps in your teeth. Long story short, you've got a choice between a toothbrush and a dentist's drill.

Underneath the enamel is the **DENTIN**. The enamel protects it, so it doesn't get a dent in. (No, come back! I promise I'll write better jokes soon!) Dentin is the scaffolding that holds your teeth together in their classic tooth shape. In the middle of every tooth is the **PULP**, which is a gooey liquid where all the nerves and blood vessels live. And right below the root, gluing it into the jaw, is the **CEMENTUM**, and I reckon you can probably work out what cementum is like.

WHY DON'T WE GET TOGETHER AND FORM A FACE?

NOSE

YOU KNOW THIS GUY: sits on the front of your face with a couple of nostrils at the bottom, and a finger inside it half the time. You might have noticed that the skeletons in this book don't have proper noses—do you know why? It's because Henry, the illustrator, is extremely lazy and can't be bothered to draw them. Not really—it's because the nose is mostly made out of something called cartilage, which is a *bit* like bone, but much more flexible. Press your nose with your finger. Now press your forehead—see the difference? (Henry is extremely lazy, though. He didn't even use color in his pictures. *Tsk*.)

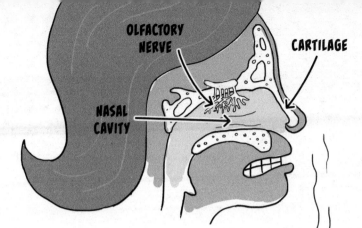

OLFACTORY NERVE

CARTILAGE

NASAL CAVITY

Separating your two nostrils is your septum, which is also made of cartilage so it can move around (in case you want to change things up and put a wider finger in there).

I've spoken to your lungs, and they told me that your nose is their favorite way for you to breathe. This is because your nose is lined with hair that stops any dirt from getting into your lungs. I know you don't particularly want to think about nose hair, but it's much better than if you had mouth hair—you'd be constantly brushing bits of pasta out of it. Your nose is one of the only parts of your body that keeps getting bigger your entire life.

It doesn't grow deliberately, but the cartilage sags a bit with gravity and your nose gets longer. Your nose also gets much bigger if you lie, but only if you're a puppet who's been carved out of wood by an Italian carpenter.

NOSE JOBS

I don't mean nose jobs as in the operations some people have to change the shape of their noses, I mean the jobs your nose does.

SMELLING

Top of the list is smelling. You might wonder how you smell, and the answer is very simple. You smell terrible. (Sorry, I couldn't resist.) Inside your nose, right at the very top of the nasal cavity, are a bunch of sensors that detect all the various perfumes and odors around you. Once you've sniffed something, the **OLFACTORY NERVE** whizzes the information to your brain, which tells you whether or not you need to stick a clothespin on your nose.

Your nose can tell the difference between a trillion different smells. A trillion is ten times the number of people who have lived on Earth since the start of time. That's 1,000,000,000,000 separate whiffs—and I bet your feet are the worst smell of all.

190

SNOT

I'm sure you're finding all this nose chat fascinating, but let's get to the real reason you're here: snot. If your nose's main job is smelling, then its second job is making snot. Snot is actually very important—it's a thin layer of sticky gunk that your nose lines itself with so it can trap any bits of dust or pollution that are lurking in the air. Some of this mucus will find its way down to the bottom of your nostrils and dry up in the air—this is known as boogers or delicious midmorning snacks.

I could tell you that you shouldn't really eat your boogers because of the horrible germs and stuff that are trapped in them, and that you might damage your nose by sticking your fingers inside, but who am I kidding? You're probably still going to do it anyway. And when grown-ups tell you off for it, remember that nine out of ten adults admit to doing it too. And the tenth one is probably lying. While there are no specific benefits to eating boogers (they don't contain any vitamins, sorry), they probably won't do you any harm either. I mean, I wouldn't recommend them as your main source of food. Just wash your hands before and after, and don't rummage around like you're trying to dig to Australia. Oh, and never offer to make me a sandwich.

If you're ill, or allergic to something, or if it's cold outside, your nose increases its production of mucus. When that happens, sometimes snot will trickle out the end of your nose, like an overflowing bath. Hopefully, it will find its way into a tissue (but more realistically, it will find its way onto the sleeve of your jacket).

SNEEZING

If your nose detects something that shouldn't be there, it fires a quick message off to your brain, which tells the muscles in your chest to quickly force air out of your nose. (I'm talking about sneezing, by the way.) If a sneeze is on its way, then it's important to let it out (ideally into a tissue). If you stop a sneeze from coming out, it can sometimes have some pretty serious consequences, like a burst eardrum, damage to blood vessels in your eye, or even a broken rib . . . and I'm sure you don't want any of those. *Aaaa-choo!*

NOSEBLEEDS

Luckily, our blood has the good sense to stay inside our bodies most of the time. Sometimes, though, it tries to escape out our nostrils. It might be because there's dry air irritating the lining of your nose, or it might be because you've got a cold, or it could be that a rogue football has clonked you in the face. But most of the time it's because you've had your finger up there. Nosebleeds are generally not a major problem, but if they happen you should find an adult so that they can help you, and so you can bleed on them instead of on yourself. They'll get you to sit down in a chair and lean your head forward to stop the blood from going down your throat, because it doesn't taste good (unless your surname is Dracula). They'll then pinch your nose just over half the way up, and hold their hand there for ten minutes, which is usually enough time to stop your blood from redecorating the floor.

Women have a much better sense of smell than men. And some people have no sense of smell at all—this is called **anosmia**.

KAY'S KWESTIONS
EXTENDED EDITION (YOU'RE WELCOME)

WHY DO I HAVE TWO EYES?

Because you'd look silly with twelve. Oh, and it also means you can see in 3D. Because each eye is in a different position on your head, they send slightly different pictures to your brain—you can see this by

The computer shop says there's so much vomit under the key they're going to have to order a new one.

closing one eye and then the other. By combining these two images, your brain is able to tell how far away things are. And we don't want you walking into walls, now, do we?

WHAT IS COLOR BLINDNESS?

Color blindness is a condition that makes it difficult to identify certain colors. The most common form of color blindness means that people can't tell the difference between red and green, which might explain why they dressed up as Little Green Riding Hood on Halloween. Color blindness usually happens because people have been born without some of their cones (those receptors in the retina that detect color). Color blindness is very common, affecting 300 million people in the world (and mostly men).

WHAT ARE THOSE WEIRD THINGS I CAN SEE IN FRONT OF MY EYES SOMETIMES?

They're called teachers. Oh, you mean the floaty little specks or squiggly lines that you sometimes see sliding around? For once, it's not a disgusting answer, like worms crawling in to eat your brain. They're known as floaters. They're very common and they're usually nothing to get stressed about—you're probably seeing little bits of your vitreous humor harmlessly moving around inside your eye. But if you're worried about anything to do with your vision, always speak to an adult.

HOW DO WE SPEAK?

When we breathe out, the air goes through a part of the windpipe called the voice box. This is where your vocal cords live, and when they vibrate they make a noise (exactly the same way that strings on a violin do). Then it's over to your tongue and your lips to wobble around and turn this noise into speech. For example, if you want to make a "b" sound, then your lips need to press together. For an "uh" sound, they need to be open in a circle, and to do the letter t they also need to press together. There, you just said "butt."

WHY DO WE HAVE BAD BREATH IN THE MORNING?

I know you're not supposed to pick on people who are smaller than you, but I'm going to have to blame bacteria for this. When we're awake, the saliva that swishes around our mouths washes the bacteria away, but at night saliva takes a break, so the bacteria run riot, making your breath as bad as Pippin's. Now, where did I leave my toothbrush?

WHAT IS A DECIBEL?

A decibel is the unit we use to measure sound, just like a meter is the unit we use to measure length. It's named after Alexander Graham Bell, who invented the telephone. His name is also why some people say "I'll give you a ring," meaning they'll call you. (It's lucky he wasn't called Alexander Graham Poo; otherwise sound would be measured in decipoos.) The higher the number of decibels, the louder the noise. A whisper is about 20 decibels, a normal conversation is 60 decibels, a train going through the station is 80 decibels, and someone shouting is 90 decibels. Anything over 85 decibels can do damage to your hearing, so next time your teacher shouts at you, you can tell them that they're endangering your health. You're welcome. Don't forget to take this book with you to read in detention.

WHY DO YOU HEAR THE OCEAN WHEN YOU HOLD A SEASHELL TO YOUR EAR?

You don't. You're just hearing the same sound as you did before, but it's now bouncing around the inside the shell, which is what makes it sound so different. It does sound a bit like the ocean, though, I'll admit.

TRUE OR POO?

YOUR EYES SEE EVERYTHING UPSIDE DOWN.

TRUE The image your eyes send to your brain is upside down, with the sky at the bottom and the ground at the top. Luckily, your brain does the sensible thing and immediately flips everything the right way around so you can read things and not freak out that you're standing on the ceiling. Thanks, brain!

SITTING CLOSE TO THE TV IS BAD FOR YOUR EYES.

POO But it *is* annoying for anyone sitting behind you, so it can be dangerous for your health if they throw a pillow at your head to make you move out of the way.

SOME PEOPLE SNORE LOUDER THAN A CHAIN SAW.

TRUE Some people's snoring is louder than a lawn mower, or a vacuum, or a pop concert, or indeed a chain saw. I live with one of those people; it's a total nightmare—it sounds like a rhino farting all night. Snoring is caused by parts of the mouth, such as the palate and the tongue, vibrating during sleep when air rushes past them.

IF YOU SNEEZE WITH YOUR EYES OPEN, THEN YOUR EYES WILL POP OUT.

POO Most people automatically close their eyes when they sneeze, but nothing bad will happen if you don't. Your eyelids aren't *that* strong—if your eyeballs were determined to fly out of their sockets, your little lids would be powerless to stop them.

THIS NEVER HAPPENS:

IT'S POSSIBLE TO HEAR COLORS AND SMELL WORDS.

TRUE Some people have a condition called synesthesia, which means some of their senses are muddled up. It's not common, but it's definitely real. Check the calendar—it's not the first of April. (Unless you're reading this on the first of April, in which case you'll just have to believe me.)

SNAKES HEAR USING THEIR TAILS.

POO Hearing with their tails? Utterly ridiculous. No, snakes actually hear with their jawbones. Their jaw picks up vibrations from the ground as they slither along your bedroom carpet. Sorry, I meant the forest floor. Definitely no snakes on your bedroom carpet. No siree.

YOU STILL HEAR THINGS WHILE YOU'RE ASLEEP.

TRUE Your body may be chilling out, but your ears don't get the night off. When you're asleep, your brain ignores most of what your ears pass on, but it still picks up some things when you've nodded off—maybe you learned something in that French lesson after all?

CHAPTER 8

BONES

WHERE WOULD YOU BE without your bones? I can tell you exactly where you'd be: on the floor, a huge sloppy bag of skin and innards sitting in a big, shapeless heap. Like Jell-O with eyes and hair. Happily, your bones are here to rescue you from a life of being a talking beanbag, so I thought you might want to get to know them a bit better.

Your skeleton doesn't just support the shape of your body; it also means you can do things like walk around, do jumping jacks, play basketball, and hit people (please don't hit people). Not only that, it's also a suit of armor to keep your squishy bits safe—it surrounds your brain, your heart, and your lungs. Without your skeleton, your brain and your heart and your lungs would all explode in a hideous, splattering mess any time you fell over (which wouldn't be great, let's be honest). Your skull hides your brain safely away, and your heart and lungs have a cage (your ribs!) protecting them. Besides keeping your organs out of harm's way and helping you move around, your bones have a surprising side gig making blood cells (you might remember me telling you this already—sorry if I've become that boring old relative who always repeats the same story). Bones are like gobstoppers, made up of lots of different layers—only a lot more disgusting. (Unless you're Pippin. She loves eating old bones. Preferably served in a muddy puddle.)

I wasn't going to list all the layers of the bone because they're a bit boring, but my friend Lee, who's an orthopedic surgeon (a bone doctor), said it was really important and I had to put them in (yawn), so here you go.

PERIOSTEUM — This is the thin (and boring—thanks a bunch, Lee) outer layer of the bone. It's where the bone's blood vessels and nerves live. How riveting.

COMPACT BONE — The next layer is called the compact bone. It might as well be called the boring bone.

CANCELLOUS BONE — Let's go a layer deeper, and it's the boring old cancellous bone. It's a little spongier, with gaps inside. A bit like a Crunch bar.

BONE MARROW — This is the gloopy layer right in the middle of your bones that makes your blood cells. Name a type of blood cell, and your bone marrow makes it. Red—yep! White—sure thing! Platelets—you betcha! Still slightly boring, though. All complaints to Lee, please.

Your bones also store minerals such as calcium, which comes from the milk you drink. But they're very modest—you'll never hear them boasting about all these clever things they do. Unlike the mouth—man, that one never shuts up!

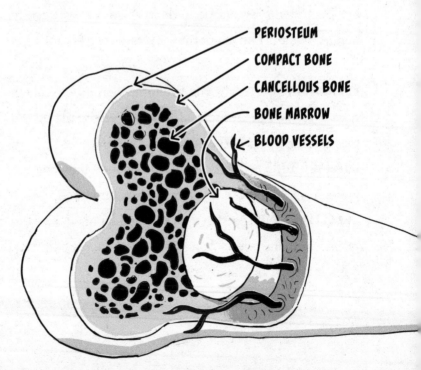

PERIOSTEUM
COMPACT BONE
CANCELLOUS BONE
BONE MARROW
BLOOD VESSELS

You are always making new bones! (Unfortunately, your skeleton never does fun things like grow wings or sprout extra arms so you can eat a sandwich while still playing computer games.) Your bones constantly clear away dusty old cells and replace them with new ones—this is why your bones can repair themselves if they break. Every five years, your body has completely replaced its entire skeleton.

SKULL

You might think your skull is just a big, boring, bony football, but it's actually made up of twenty-two different bones, all stitched together to make your beautiful/ stupid head (delete as appropriate, depending on whether you have a beautiful head or a stupid one). You'll be pleased to hear that most of these twenty-two bones are firmly glued in place, keeping your brain safely locked away . . . all except one bone, which loves to move around. Any ideas? Yes, you at the back with the terrible haircut. That's right—the jaw! The jaw (or the mandible, as it likes to be known professionally) is a hinged marvel that can move freely so you can chew your food and yabber away about how brilliant this book is and how it's totally changed your life.

SPINE TIME

Coming down from your skull is your spine, also known as your backbone, also known as your กระดูกสันหลัง (if you speak Thai). It's a very clever bit of engineering—the spine needs to be extremely strong (to keep your body standing up, protect your precious spinal cord, and hold up your big old head) but also extremely bendy (so you can tie your shoelaces, and your uncle can dance really badly at Christmas). To do this, it's made up of lots of little bones called vertebrae—thirty-three of them, in fact—all slotted together like a Lego snake.

The seven bones at the top of your spine are called your **CERVICAL VERTEBRAE**. Any guesses what "cervical" means? It begins with n. . . . That's right: nincompoop. No, sorry—I got that wrong. I meant neck.

When you were born, you had about 300 bones, and you have fewer and fewer bones every year until you're fully grown and you're left with only 206. Yes, really. And no, they weren't stolen from you in the night by a terrifying bone-eating monster. (Probably.) No, they're still in there—they've just joined forces, fusing together to form bigger bones. It's a bit like when a bag of chocolates melts and then cools down to make one big mega-chocolate.

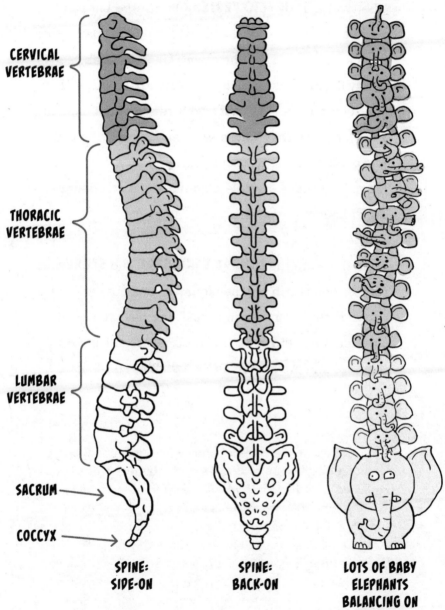

CERVICAL
VERTEBRAE

THORACIC
VERTEBRAE

LUMBAR
VERTEBRAE

SACRUM →

COCCYX →

SPINE:
SIDE-ON

SPINE:
BACK-ON

LOTS OF BABY
ELEPHANTS
BALANCING ON
THEIR MOM

The twelve **THORACIC VERTEBRAE** are the ones in the middle attached to your ribs, which are the protective packaging around your heart and lungs. Your rib cage is pretty flexible: take a really deep breath in and see how your chest puffs out. That's your ribs making room for your lungs as they fill up with air. If your ribs didn't move out of the way, they might puncture one of your lungs, and that's a whole nightmare you can definitely do without.

Then there are the **LUMBAR VERTEBRAE** and **SACRUM** at the bottom, which are the bit grown-ups put their hand on when they yell, 'Oh, my back!' and have to lie down. The four vertebrae at the bottom are all joined together and are known as the **COCCYX**. The coccyx

The longest and strongest bone in the human body is the thigh bone, known to doctors as the **femur**. (Not to be confused with the lemur, which lives in trees in Madagascar. You probably wouldn't have gotten them confused, actually—they're pretty different.) The long old femur starts at your hip and goes all the way down to your knee. The smallest bone in your body is called the stapes—which you met in the last chapter—hiding deep down inside your ear. It's only the size of a grain of rice, so try not to lose it!

helps you keep your balance when you're sitting down, but it used to be much more interesting. The humble coccyx is, I am excited to reveal, all that remains of your tail. Yes! You used to have a tail. Well, not you personally, and not anyone else in your family. (Apart from that aunt with the green scaly skin who has a really long tongue and eats insects.) I mean millions of years ago. These days, nature has decided that, since we don't do much swinging off trees anymore, we don't really need a tail—so all we've got left is the coccyx. Very unfair, if you ask me. (I'd mostly use mine to waft away farts.)

Giraffes and humans have exactly the same number of vertebrae in their necks. The giraffe's are just a teensy-weensy bit bigger. (Okay, fine, they're massively bigger.)

Your legs don't just connect into the bottom of the spine (unless you're a stick figure, in which case I guess they do). Your spine and your legs both join into a weird Lifesaver candy of bone called the pelvis. It's the shape of a Lifesaver candy, by the way, not the flavor. Actually . . . I've never tried eating one before. Maybe your pelvis is delicious and fruity too.

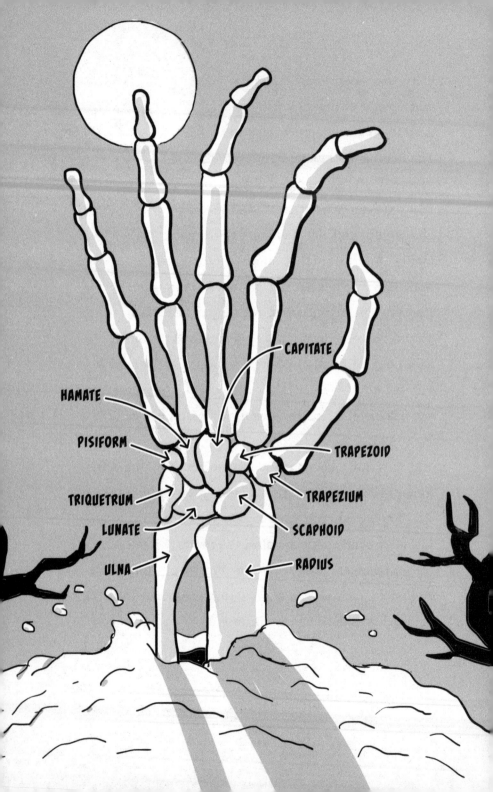

CAPITATE

HAMATE

PISIFORM

TRIQUETRUM

LUNATE

ULNA

TRAPEZOID

TRAPEZIUM

SCAPHOID

RADIUS

HANDS

Your hands have *soooo* many bones in them—really sorry about that, it's loads for you to learn. Your wrist alone is made up of eight bones (known as the carpal bones), each with their own weird name: **SCAPHOID**, **LUNATE**, **TRIQUETRUM**, **PISIFORM** (no laughing), **HAMATE**, **CAPITATE**, **TRAPEZIUM**, and **TRAPEZOID**. Even doctors find it difficult remembering them all. Here's how I do it, taking the first letter of each bone: **S**top **L**icking **T**hat **P**oo, **H**orrible **C**hild. **T**ut **T**ut.

Then there are the bones in the palm of your hand, also known as the **METACARPALS**. Clive and his naming committee clearly weren't feeling particularly imaginative when they were naming those parts, so they're called the first, second, third, fourth, and fifth metacarpals. If you make a fist, the five knuckles that stick out are the ends of your metacarpals. Now unmake that fist, please—you're scaring me.

KAY
TERRIBLE AUTHOR

PAKER
EXCELLENT
ARTIST

THUMB — All your other fingers have three bones each (called phalanges, if you care), but your thumb only has two. What it lacks in the bone department, though, it more than makes up for in other ways. It's the strongest digit in your hand, it can move in more directions than any other, and it's the one you use the most. Think of something you do with your hands, and it probably involves your thumb. Okay, fine—not picking your nose. But you use it for eating, climbing, writing, and flicking the ear of whoever's sitting in front of you.

INDEX FINGER — This one can do the most delicate movements, so it's the finger you use to guide your pen when you're writing or drawing. It's also the only finger I use for typing. You wouldn't believe how long it took me to write this book.

MIDDLE FINGER — It's mostly used alongside other fingers—for example, with your thumb if you want to snap your fingers. It's sometimes used on its own, though—for example, by your parents when they're driving and someone nearly crashes into them.

RING FINGER — People have put their engagement and wedding rings on this finger for thousands of years—it's because of an ancient belief that there was a vein in the ring finger that ran directly to the heart. Not only is this nonsense, but the heart doesn't have anything to do with love, since it's just a big, gory lump of muscle. Your ring finger uses the same internal mechanism (called tendons) as your middle finger, so it's not as independent as your other fingers. Want me to prove it? Put your hand flat down on a table, then bend your middle finger underneath so it's touching your palm. Now try to lift up your ring finger. See—it won't move. Stupid ring finger.

PINKY FINGER — It might be small, but it's mighty. In fact, your pinky provides about half of your hand's strength. If you ever have to choose one of your fingers to chop off, don't go for your little finger. Scientists actually think lopping off your index finger would have the least effect on your life. (Luckily, I can't imagine a situation where you'd have to make this choice!)

If you stretch out your arms as far as they can go, then take a tape measure to see how wide that is, it will be about the same as your height. Cool, right? And if you take that tape measure and wrap it five times around your head, then you'll look like an idiot.

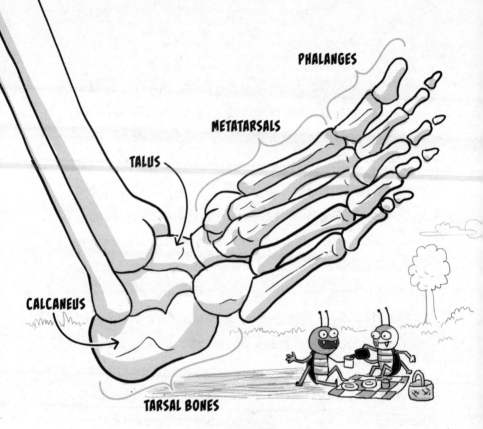

PHALANGES

METATARSALS

TALUS

CALCANEUS

TARSAL BONES

FEET

Your poor feet don't have the most glamorous of lives, do they? Hidden away in your shoes and cursed to always have a bit of a whiff about them. Plus we slam the entire weight of our bodies onto them thousands of times a day. Your feet are actually a lot more complex than you might think—each one is made up of twenty-six bones, thirty-three joints, and over one hundred muscles and tendons.

The average
person walks over
100,000 miles in their
lifetime—that's the same as
walking around the world
four times. I hope you're
wearing comfortable
shoes.

At the back of your foot are seven tarsal bones, including your ankle bone (called the **TALUS**) and your heel bone (or **CALCANEUS**). In front of those, you have five metatarsals a bit like the **METACARPALS** in your hand. Then, at the front of your foot, there are your toes. Similar to your fingers, all your toes have three bones, apart from your big toe, which for some reason isn't called your foot thumb.

JOINTS

You know the song that says the head bone's connected to the neck bone, and the neck bone's connected to the shoulder bone, and the shoulder bone's connected to the backbone . . .? Well, medically it's total nonsense: that'll teach you to learn anatomy from song lyrics. Thank goodness I'm here.

**PIVOT
JOINT**

**BALL-AND-
SOCKET
JOINT**

**HINGE
JOINT**

Where one bone connects with another bone, it's called a joint, and you've got almost four hundred of them in your body. Lucky you! There are various types of joints, such as the **HINGE JOINT**, which you can find in your knees. Hinge joints open and close like a door, using—you've guessed it—a hinge. Instead of needing oil to keep its hinges moving easily, your body lubricates its joints with synovial fluid, which looks a bit like egg white. Your body makes synovial fluid whenever you need it, so you don't have to wander round with a can of it, squirting it into your knees whenever they start to squeak.

Other types of joints are a bit more complicated. Your hips, for example, need to move in more than one direction, or you'd only be able to walk around like a soldier on parade and you'd never win at Twister. They use a system called a **BALL-AND-SOCKET JOINT**, which consists of a ball and a . . . you're way ahead of me. This means that your legs can go backward and forward, side to side, and even in a circle. Next time you're playing soccer you can thank your ball-and-socket joints. (And next time your uncle is dancing around the living room at Christmas, you can blame his.)

Quick! Look to your left! There's a tarantula the size of a house running over to eat you! There's not really (hopefully), but when you turned your head you used a **PIVOT JOINT** in your neck. A pivot joint is designed to swivel around, and it works like an onion ring on a hot dog. (Try one—it's delicious!)

You know how some people have an annoying habit of bending their knuckles until they make a cracking sound? That horrible noise comes from little bubbles of air inside the synovial fluid. Some people say that cracking your joints can lead to arthritis (we'll come to arthritis in a minute), but that's not actually true. People only pretend it's true because the noise makes them feel sick, so they want you to stop doing it. *C-R-A-C-K!* Ah, that's better.

If a joint becomes dislocated, that means it's popped out of its normal position and can't move around properly. This sometimes happens because you've injured yourself—for example, if you bounce off a trampoline and land on your shoulder. Ouch. It might pop back in on its own, or you might need your robot butler to take you to the hospital and get it put back in place—but if you want my advice, it's best to avoid dislocating things in the first place. Right, it's time for my trampoline class.

There's more to your joints than just bones. You also have ligaments, which hold everything together—they're basically the body's elastic bands. Ligament damage is one of the most common injuries that happen to professional athletes. (Apart from boxers. The most common injury for boxers is being punched in the face.)

You might have a friend who says they're double-jointed because they can bend their thumb halfway to their elbow or lick their own back. They don't actually have any more joints than you or me; they've got something called hypermobility, which means their ligaments are a bit stretchier, so they can fold themselves up like a pretzel.

BROKEN BONES

Sticks and stones may break my bones . . . and this is what happens if they do.

Even though bones are tough old things, unfortunately they can still break sometimes. Unless you're Superman. In fact, skip this whole section if you're Superman. Because bones are always replacing their cells, they're able to do a pretty decent repair job on themselves. By the way, a fracture is the same as a broken bone—some people think that a fracture is a kind of minor break, but it's just the doctory word for exactly the same thing.

X-rays were invented over a hundred years ago by Wilhelm Röntgen, a professor in Germany. He originally called his discovery Roentgenology, but it didn't really catch on and now everyone calls them X-rays—sorry, Wilhelm! Knowing how to treat broken bones is much, much older, though. In fact, the ancient Egyptians wrote about how to do it over three thousand years ago!

X-RAY

The only exciting thing about breaking a bone is having an X-ray. (Although still not worth it—trust me, I've broken three ankles. I mean, I've broken an ankle three times. I've only got two ankles.) A radiographer (X-ray specialist) will point an X-ray machine at whichever bone they're worried about, and it will shine X-rays through you. Yes, *through you*. X-rays are a special type of light that you can't see—they zoom painlessly through your skin and your flesh and your muscles and whatnot, and pop out the other side. Your softer bits appear black and gray, but because your bones are a lot more solid, X-rays don't go through them, so they look white. And, hey presto, a picture of your bones, showing if there's a break.

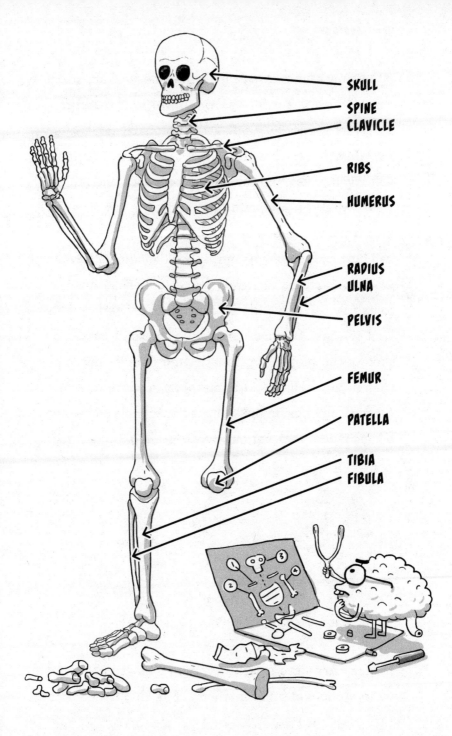

SKULL

SPINE
CLAVICLE

RIBS

HUMERUS

RADIUS
ULNA

PELVIS

FEMUR

PATELLA

TIBIA
FIBULA

If the X-ray says there's a break, then the most important thing to do is to put the picture up on Instagram immediately. Actually, you should probably get treated by a doctor or a nurse first. Most of the time, treatment just involves keeping the broken bone nice and still for a few weeks. If a bone moves around, it won't repair properly, and can end up all wonky. Plus, broken bones can hurt *a lot* when you move them. You might have to wear a sling if you've broken your collarbone (or clavicle, to its friends). Other breaks might mean wearing a big boot or a cast. Besides keeping the bone still, casts also protect the broken bit from getting injured any more than it already is. Most importantly, a cast gives your friends something to draw all over, or scribble bad words on, or make very serious written allegations about whose farts are the smelliest.

X-rays are the simplest way to look at bones, but there are lots of other methods of looking inside your body—for example, **CT** scans (short for computed tomography, if you care) and **MRI**s (magnetic resonance imaging—you don't care, do you?). CT scans and MRIs both involve lying very still in a plastic tunnel while it takes pictures of your insides. CT scanners use a type of X-ray, and MRI scanners use very powerful magnets. It's important not to wear a watch when you have an MRI, because the magnet is so strong that your watch would fly off your wrist and get stuck to the scanner. It's even more important that you not have any bits of metal inside your body if you have an MRI, because they would rip out of your body and . . . No, that's too revolting, even for *this* book.

Very rarely, a bone is so badly broken that the two (or three or fifteen) bits won't come together on their own, and you need an operation. This usually involves putting special metal pins or rods inside to hold everything together. On the downside, it's never any fun having an operation and it'll be a while until you're totally better. On the upside, you'll *BEEP* every time you go through one of those scanners at the airport, and you can explain to the security guard that there's some cool metalwork inside your leg, so you're technically half human and half machine.

Some people are born without arms, or legs, or both. And some people lose their limbs in accidents or because of illness. These days, it's possible to use artificial (also known as prosthetic) arms and legs. There are even prosthetic limbs that pick up brainwaves so they know exactly how to move.

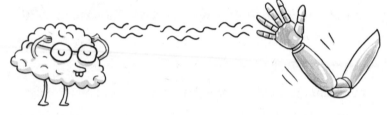

Athletes with prosthetic legs can run almost as fast as those who have the legs they were born with. As technology is getting better all the time, it won't be long before people with prosthetic legs are the fastest athletes on earth!

ARTHRITIS

An -*itis* means a part of your body is inflamed and swollen. For example, we've already talked about conjunctivitis (which means your conjunctiva is inflamed) and tonsillitis (which means your tonsils are). But what's your arth? No, not that. Arth means your joints. Arthritis is mostly something that affects older people, and makes their joints painful and stiff. Although it's not common, some young people can get a kind of arthritis called juvenile arthritis or JIA. Physiotherapy is very helpful for people with juvenile arthritis, and there are also anti-inflammatory medications available that reduce the symptoms.

KAY'S KWESTIONS

HOW MANY BONES ARE IN MY HANDS?

You have fifty-four bones in your hands (twenty-seven in each). If you add that to the fifty-two bones in your feet that's over half of the bones in

The shop has ordered a new key, but it's being sent from Australia, so I'll just have to wait for now.

your whole body! A bit greedy, if you ask me.

WHY DO WE STOP GROWING?

How tall you grow has nothing to do with eating the crusts of your bread or your greens. Yep, I'm afraid you may have been fibbed to about that one. (Although eating vegetables is still extremely important for the strength of your bones. Apologies—I can't offer you a completely broccoli-free life.) The height you grow to is pretty much decided the day you're born—and it's mostly determined by the height of your biological parents. Blame them if you always wanted to be a superstar basketball player the height of a house. Your hormones tell your bones to stop growing when they reach the size they're meant to be—usually when you're about eighteen—and that's as tall as you're going to get.

HOW MANY RIBS DO I HAVE?

I don't know, sorry . . . You *probably* have twelve pairs of ribs (so twenty-four in total), but some people are the proud owners of a thirteenth pair—a tiny little extra set right up at the top. Extra ribs can be a real pain in the neck. (Literally—they cause neck pain.)

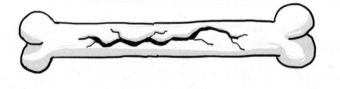

TRUE OR POO?

YOU'RE SHORTER AT NIGHT THAN YOU ARE IN THE MORNING.

TRUE After a full day's stomping around, your vertebrae end up pressing down into each other a little bit. When you go to bed, your spine stretches out and replenishes its synovial fluid. Just like a hamburger with more toppings is bigger, all this extra fluid between your vertebrae means your spine becomes taller too. About a centimeter or so, to be precise. I don't know if you've ever been to space, but if you have then you'll remember that when you were up there you were taller than ever, with no gravity to squash your spine downward.

EVERY BONE IS CONNECTED TO ANOTHER BONE.

POO But only just. There's one stubborn bone that refuses to hang with the rest of the crowd, called the hyoid. This V-shaped loner lives at the base of your tongue and is one of the bunch of body bits involved in helping you speak.

YOUR FUNNY BONE IS THE BIGGEST BONE IN YOUR ARM.

POO It's not even a bone at all. Sometimes when you bang your elbow it gives you a tingling sensation, which is known as "hitting your funny bone." But that feeling actually comes from clonking a nerve called the ulnar nerve. The bone in your upper arm is called the humerus. Hmmm, say that out loud. "Humerus." Sounds a bit like "humorous"—maybe that's where the term "funny bone" comes from? Classic Clive.

VERY HUMERUS.

LET'S TALK ABOUT MUSCLES. You probably only think about the ones bulging out of people who spend every minute of their life in the gym, or the ones stretching out Superman's onesie. But there's a lot more to muscles than looking buff or fighting off bad guys with one arm while lifting up a jumbo jet with the other. The truth is, without the 600 muscles dotted inside our bodies, we wouldn't be able to do much at all. And I'm not just talking about ballet dancing, wiggling your ears, waggling your eyebrows, and sticking your tongue out. Breathing uses muscles, eating uses muscles, even your heart is a muscle—without your muscles you couldn't live (so please don't sell them on eBay).

The word muscle comes from the Latin word **musculus,** which means "little mouse." This is because the Romans thought that muscles looked like little mice crawling under the skin. Yuck.

Let's say you want to go for a run, or pick your nose, or run away from someone who's picking their nose. Anything like that involves lots of muscles moving together, and there's one part of the body that makes it all work, like the conductor of an orchestra. That's right: the butt. Sorry, my mistake—I meant the brain. I must remember to delete that sentence later. Your brain sends a message down through your nerves at lightning speed, all the way to each muscle it wants to get moving. When a muscle receives this message, each of its cells gets shorter . . . and this means the whole muscle tightens up. If that muscle is attached to a bone, like in your arm, for example, then the bone moves. Look, you're waving!

WHAT YOUR MUSCLES DO

MOVING

This is your muscles' main job. It's what they put in the "about me" section of their social media profiles.

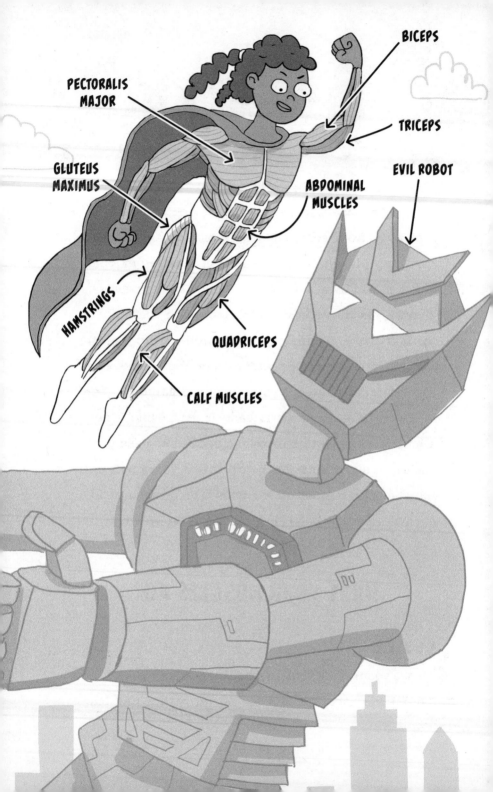

They pull your bones around, and that makes you move. The type of muscle that does all this is known as skeletal muscle, because it's attached to your skeleton. You've got loads of bones and organs and things to carry around (no offense), so you need a lot of skeletal muscle—in fact, almost half of your weight is made up of skeletal muscle. If you found all of someone's skeletal muscle lying in a pile on the ground it would be much too heavy for you to pick up. (If you *do* find all of someone's skeletal muscle lying in a pile on the ground, you should call the police right away—it sounds like quite a horrific crime has been committed.)

The walking and pointing and climbing you do all day is hard work for your poor muscles, so they need a good night's sleep, which is when they can finally go floppy and recharge. That's why it's important to sleep in a bed, so you can be totally flat and your muscles can get a proper rest. If you fall asleep in a chair or at your school desk (we've all been there), then your muscles will snooze in the wrong position and they'll feel painful when you wake up.

WHY DON'T WE GET TO WEAR CAPES?

233

I know you're not supposed to have favorites (although Pippin is my favorite dog in the world, even though she was sick in my cereal this morning), but here are a few of my top muscles:

The fastest muscles in your body are the ones in your eye—they're constantly moving tiny amounts, so that you're always looking in the right direction. In the ten seconds it took you to read that last sentence, your eyes moved about thirty times. No wonder they feel tired at the end of the day!

BICEPS — These are the muscles that bend your elbows and pull up your forearms (that's the half of your arm nearer your hand). I like this muscle because it's the one I use to move chocolate from the fridge to my face. When people exercise with weights a lot, biceps are the ones in the arms that bulge out like someone's put tennis balls under their skin.

TRICEPS — This is a huge dinosaur with three horns and an enormous tail. No, hang on—that's a triceratops. Your triceps are the muscles on the back of your arms that straighten your elbows—the opposite of their buddies, the biceps. Because muscles can only move things in one direction, they often work in pairs like this. (These are called antagonistic muscles, if you were worrying I haven't taught you enough long words recently.)

QUADRICEPS — You can call them quads if you like—they're cool with it. These are the big muscles on the front of your thighs that move your knees.

NOT A HAMSTRING

234

Professional cyclists have massive quads (and a very sore butt from sitting on a bike seat all day).

HAMSTRINGS — Nope, not something you might find on a guitar made of bacon. Your hamstrings are the muscles at the back of your leg that do the opposite movement of your quads.

NOT HAMSTRINGS

CALF MUSCLES — These hang out at the back of your legs, underneath your hamstrings, and pull up the heels of your feet, making them very important for walking. They're particularly useful for walking on your tiptoes, so make sure you train these muscles if you want to be a burglar when you grow up.

PECTORALIS MAJOR — Your pectoralis majors (or pecs, to their friends) are the muscles in your upper chest that help your shoulders move, so they're particularly important if you want to do the Macarena.

GLUTEUS MAXIMUS — There's a fancy Latin name for almost every part of your body, and your butt is no exception. Your butt, my butt, the queen's butt—they all contain the gluteus maximus. And give that butt a medal—your gluteus maximus is the largest muscle in your body!

ALSO NOT HAMSTRINGS

STAPEDIUS — The smallest muscle in your body is in your ear—in fact, it's connected to the smallest bone in your body! It's called the stapedius and it's only the size of this period. ←

PROTECTION

You might think that protecting your innards is your bones' department, but your muscles are also part of your body's force field. There aren't any bones protecting your tummy, so it's over to your muscles—your abdominal muscles, to be specific, aka your abs, aka your six-pack. If you touch your tummy, your abs are there to stop your finger from prodding anything it shouldn't, like your liver or intestines.

You know when your teachers tell you "Stand up straight!" or "Don't slouch!" or "Why have you covered Susan in jam?!" Well, if they'd read this book, they would actually be telling you to tighten your abdominal muscles, because doing that and pushing your shoulders back is how to improve your posture. (They would probably still tell you not to cover Susan in jam.) Using your muscles to stand up straight is important because

YOU NEED TO WORK ON YOUR POSTURE.

IT'S FINE.

236

you're less likely to have pain in your joints and muscles when you're older if you do. Sorry—your teachers aren't just nagging you for no reason.

BREATHING

I don't know about you, but I always think breathing is a pretty important part of my day, and none of it would happen without the diaphragm. The diaphragm isn't one of your skeletal muscles—it's a different type, known as smooth muscle because it always wears stylish clothing. (Actually, it's because of what its cells look like under a microscope.) Smooth muscles don't need your body to tell them to move—they just get on with it. And thank goodness they do—it would be a real pain if you had to remember to breathe every few seconds. Your brain stem just chats away with your smooth muscles in the background, without bothering you about it. That way, you can get on with thinking about more important things, like watching TV, eating hot dogs, and plotting to overthrow your teacher.

EATING AND POOPING

Every stage of digestion involves muscles—from the moment food goes into your mouth until the moment it splashes into the toilet. Your jaw muscles do the chewing;

then some other ones squeeze it down to your stomach (which is a big bag of muscle itself); then even more muscles help it through your intestines and all the way to your butt. And when you get that twitch that tells you it's time to go to the bathroom because something's coming, well, that's a muscle too.

TEMPERATURE

If you're too cold (for example, if you're wearing an outfit made out of ice pops), then your muscles have an ingenious plan. They quickly tighten, then relax, then tighten, then relax, and this heats up your body. You might know this better as shivering! Every time a muscle tightens or relaxes, it creates heat—that's why people lifting weights in the gym turn such a lovely shade of beet red.

HEART

I probably don't need to remind you how important your heart is, or that it's made of muscle, but it's on the list because I don't want to upset it.

EXERCISE

Phones and computer games and TVs are obviously wonderful . . . but we're using them so much these days that we're doing less exercise than any humans in all of history. Exercise is really important. It makes your lungs and your heart strong, plus it decreases your chances of developing illnesses later in life. It also makes you sleep better and feel happier—what's not to like? Scientists say that you should spend at least an hour every day doing some physical activity. It needs to be something that makes your heart beat faster—so picking up a remote control doesn't count. Easy things you can do every day for exercise include walking, jogging, cycling, skateboarding, and fighting an enormous zombie dinosaur that's trying to destroy your city.

If you've been exercising particularly hard, then your muscles might feel sore afterward. This is because you've caused lots of tiny rips in your muscle fibers. But it won't make your leg fall off. (Probably.) When those little rips heal, your muscles will become bigger and stronger. In fact, you've got the same number of muscles in your arms and legs as a weightlifter—theirs are just bigger. Muscles need protein to rebuild, which is why protein is a really important part of your diet. Right, get exercising! Superman will be quaking in his cape very soon.

YOUR FACE

Unless you're an identical twin or you've been cloned by a supervillain who's trying to take over the world, your face is totally unique. It can make hundreds of different expressions, from raising an eyebrow at your uncle's terrible jokes to sticking your tongue out at him (behind his back, obviously). Unlike your skeletal muscles, which link bones to other bones, your facial muscles are attached to your skull at one end and your skin at the other end, pulling it in all sorts of different directions.

FACIAL EXPRESSIONS

HAPPY   **SAD**   **EVIL**

CUTE   **TOO CUTE**   **TOO MUCH TV**

SHIFTY   **SNOOTY**   **SNOTTY**

SLEEPY   **ANGRY**   **ZOMBIFIED**

Not everyone has the same number of muscles in their face—some people have loads more! That friend of yours who can make you scream with laughter because his face twists and turns like it's made of plastic probably has extra muscles, and people who have naturally gloomy expressions are often missing them. Maybe we should arrange a fundraiser to get teachers a few more smile muscles?

It's amazing (and also kind of gross) to think of these thin, stretchy muscles in there yanking your skin around to make you smile or sneer or screw up your face.

SPRAINS AND STRAINS

If you slip and twist your ankle, or if you stop yourself from falling by putting your hands out, or if you lift a fridge over your head, then you might find yourself with a sprain or a strain. This means that you've hurt a muscle, or one of your ligaments or tendons. You might remember that ligaments join bones to other bones—well, tendons are little straps that join muscles to bones. ("Tendons" can, of course, also mean ten people named Don.) Your body is very good at repairing sprains and strains, and they usually get back to normal much quicker than broken bones. You treat your poor sore, swollen joint by thinking of RICE.

Rest – Chill out on the sofa for a bit.

Ice – Your robot butler needs to go to the freezer and get you a bag of frozen peas and a tub of ice cream. The frozen peas should be wrapped in a dish towel and put on the injury to help the swelling go down. The ice cream is for you to eat.

Compression – Wrap a bandage around the injury.

Elevate – Raise it up on a pillow.

CRAMPS

Ouch! What's going on? One of your muscles has suddenly decided to lock up tight for no good reason! It might be because you've been sitting awkwardly, or you've been using the muscle a lot. Or sometimes it happens for no reason at all—maybe you said something mean about that muscle and it's taking revenge?

Stretching the muscle can help, and so can getting one of your personal servants (you may know them as relatives) to massage it. And a bit more ice cream isn't going to do any harm, is it?

Your most waggle-able muscle is the tongue—although, technically, it's made of eight separate muscles. This gives the tongue its unique bendiness, stretchiness, and all-around weird tongue-ness. It's not like any other muscle in the body—in fact, it's much more similar to an octopus's tentacles or an elephant's trunk—although I know which one of those I'd rather have coming out the middle of my mouth. (Octopus tentacle, obvs.) It's also the only muscle in your body that's connected at just one end. If you find another muscle that's only connected at one end, then you should probably speak to a doctor about it pretty urgently.

KAY'S KWESTIONS

WHY DO DOCTORS BANG ON PEOPLE'S KNEES WITH A HAMMER?

Has your doctor ever taken a hammer and banged just below your knee? There are two possible reasons. The first reason is that your doctor really hates you and wants to hit you with a hammer. The second (more likely) reason is that they are checking your reflexes. A reflex is what we call an automatic reaction—something your nerves tell your muscles to do, without running it past your brain first. For example, if you accidentally touch something really hot, your body has a reflex to pull your arm away quickly without you even having to think about it. If something flicks into your eye, your body knows to make you blink. Or if something touches the back of your throat, your body automatically does a kind of unpleasant retching to get rid of anything that shouldn't be there. Anyway, back to knees. When the doctor taps this specific point underneath your knee, it makes your leg kick out, and this tells them that your reflexes are working properly. (But if they do throw a ball at your head, then that probably means they hate you.)

> The key is arriving at the shop tomorrow—I should be able to spell things normally very soon. Apologies again for this.

WHY DO PEOPLE FLY ACROSS THE ROOM WHEN THEY GET ELECTROCUTED?

Hopefully you've never been electrocuted, but maybe you've seen it happen to someone on TV—they get an electric shock and *BOOM!* Suddenly they're lying in the opposite corner of the room. This is all because of muscles. If an electric current runs through you, it makes your muscles tighten up extremely quickly and then . . . off you fly. I've been electrocuted before, and I really wouldn't recommend it. Leave the flying to birds, planes, and Superman. And if you really want to make your hair stand on end, it's much less painful to use hair gel.

HOW DO PEOPLE CHEAT IN RACES TO RUN FASTER?

You might have heard of sports stars having their medals taken away from them for cheating. Doing this is bad, not just because cheating is wrong, but because the drugs they use are very dangerous. Anabolic steroids, which are a type of drug that people use to cheat in sports, increase muscle size and strength but can lead to heart problems in later life. Cheaters are nothing new—there are reports of athletes thousands of years ago in ancient Greece being banned for taking potions to help them win their races. κακός!

TRUE OR POO?

SMILING IS CONTAGIOUS.

TRUE It isn't just horrid stuff like a cold or chicken pox
that's contagious—smiling is too. If you smile at someone,
then their brain automatically tells them to smile. The
same happens with yawning—if you let out a huge yawn,
other people in the room will yawn. . . . Try it!

YOUR FINGERS HAVE MUSCLES IN THEM.

POO This might be a bit of a surprise . . . but your
fingers are too small to contain the muscles they need
to move. If you had muscles in your fingers, they would
look like a big fat bunch of bananas and you wouldn't be
able to tie your shoelaces. Instead, your body has parked

these muscles in your wrists and at the bottom of your arms, and it moves your fingers by remote control (well, using extra-long tendons). In other words, your hand is a kind of haunted puppet.

IT TAKES MORE MUSCLES TO FROWN THAN TO SMILE.

POO This is just a myth that people say to make you smile for photographs, but the truth is it's impossible to work out how many muscles are used for smiling or frowning, because we all move our faces around using slightly different combinations of muscles. Next time someone says this to you, just stick your tongue out and say that took fewer muscles than either smiling or frowning.

TOO MUCH TIME PLAYING COMPUTER GAMES CAN DAMAGE YOUR HANDS.

TRUE I'm really sorry, I know it's not what you wanted to hear. When you play computer games a lot, you end up doing the same actions with your hands over and over again. This can cause swelling around the tendons that move your fingers and thumb, known as tendonitis. It should really be known as Nintendonitis.

CHAPTER 10
GUT

GRAB SOME RAIN BOOTS, a pair of thick plastic gloves, a waterproof jacket, and a clothespin for your nose—it's time to explore your gut. That's right—the ten yards of tubing that runs from your mouth to your . . . I'm going to have to say butthole, aren't I? Fine, Okay—the ten yards of tubing that runs from your mouth to your butthole, performing that clever magic trick of turning food into poop.

But why do we eat food? It's not just to keep the toilet-paper companies in business. Sorry to be all dramatic here, but if we don't eat, then we die. Food is the gasoline in your personal fuel tank—absolutely everything that your body does requires food. Your digestive system is like a sorting machine (except it's got slimy walls and smells terrible) that takes the food, picks out all the useful bits and bobs for your body to use as energy, then packs the rest off on its journey to the toilet.

Let's meet all the different parts of your digestive system. Well, I say "meet," I mean read about. I'm not going to make you go on a playdate with a pancreas.

THE DIGESTIVE SYSTEM

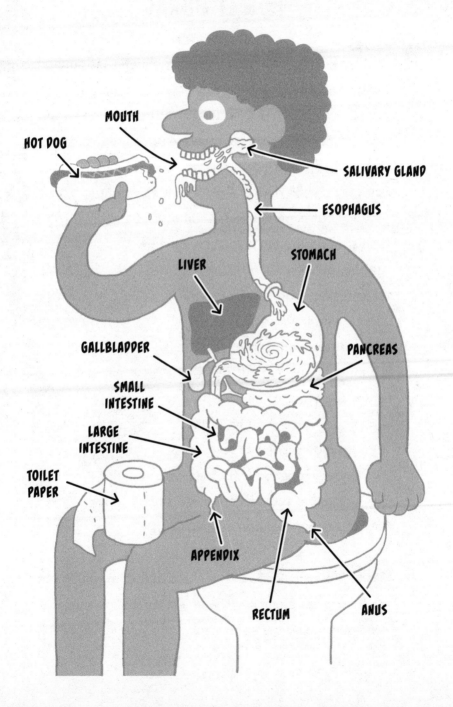

HOW IT WORKS

MOUTH — Breathing, talking, eating, singing, burping—is there anything the mouth can't do? (Yep: play tennis.) The mouth is where your food's journey begins—your teeth chew it up; then your tongue turns it into a ball of soggy goop and passes it on. Your mouth has six salivary glands dotted around that spray out spit, like a fancy but slightly repulsive shower. Saliva (which is spit's proper name) helps you swallow things, keeps germs off your teeth, and stops your mouth from drying out. It also contains enzymes, which are the chemicals that break up your food so it can be absorbed by your body (a bit like how dish soap breaks up the food my robot butler burned onto the bottom of the saucepan after his latest cooking disaster).

APOLOGIES. I HAD A FEW ISSUES IN THE KITCHEN.

ESOPHAGUS — This is the pipe that runs from your throat down to your stomach. The epiglottis makes sure that food goes down here rather than into your lungs, which have a strict air-only admissions policy. Food is squeezed down by muscles—it doesn't just slide into your stomach like it's going down a garbage chute. This means it's possible to eat food if you're hanging upside down! (Don't try this, just take my word for it.) Your esophagus has a tight ring of muscle at the bottom to stop any food or drink from sloshing back up from your stomach. Just as well; otherwise every time you tried to speak, bits of old mashed potato would come out.

The saliva you produce in a single day would fill two cans of Coke. It would be a bit less fizzy, though. Hopefully. If you've got fizzy saliva, maybe see a doctor. Or an alien investigator.

STOMACH — Your stomach is your body's very own smoothie maker. It takes the chewed-up chicken nuggets and toast and

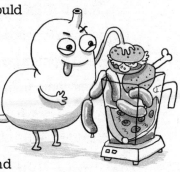

bananas that you had for lunch (a weird lunch, if you ask me) and turns it all into a liquid. It's not a very appetizing smoothie, because your stomach adds loads of really strong acid to it. Then it uses its very impressive muscles to churn the food around and around until it's all a gloopy slop, ready for your intestines, which clearly aren't fussy eaters.

SMALL INTESTINE — It's only called small because of how narrow it is. If you took your small intestine (aka small bowel) out of your body and hung it from your bedroom window, it would actually be at least four times as tall as you. Although, if you did that, you'd probably have more urgent things to worry about than how long your intestines are.

As food goes through your small intestine, it meets lots more enzymes—remember them? Each enzyme has a preferred type of food that it breaks down so your body can absorb it. Fair enough—we've all got a favorite food. (My favorite food is deep-pan pizza with onions and sweet corn, and Pippin's favorite food is old shoes.) Some of these enzymes come from an unpleasant-looking green liquid known as bile, which squirts out of a little bag called the gallbladder, and others come from a place called the pancreas. The pancreas is a small, flat organ nestled between your stomach and your small intestine, and I'll tell you a bit more about it later in this chapter. That's the sort of cliffhanger that'll keep you hooked, right? Oh.

When the enzymes have done their enzyme-y thing, the smushed-up food passes through the walls of the small intestine into the bloodstream, before heading off to the liver, where any bad stuff will get filtered out. It's now about six hours since you put it in your mouth, and what's left at the end of your small intestine is pretty unrecognizable—it looks like a watery soup that you definitely wouldn't want to be served for dinner. This disgusting minestrone passes straight through into the large intestine for the next part of its pooey journey.

Over your lifetime, you will chomp through about 30 tons of food—that's the weight of about twenty fully grown hippos. Don't eat it all at once!

LARGE INTESTINE — The large intestine (or large bowel) is essentially a factory. Some factories make computers, some factories make furniture, and some factories make sweets. This factory makes . . . poop.

POOTTERY WORKSHOP

What comes out of the small intestine has already had most of its useful nutrients taken out of it, so all that's left for its big brother to do is squeeze the water out, then let a bunch of helpful bacteria turn it into the poop that you know and love. Well, maybe not love. There's a very small tube that comes off the large intestine called your appendix, which does . . . absolutely nothing. Zero. Zilch. Useless. Your body probably just put it there so science teachers would have even more stuff to make you learn about.

The only time you'll ever know you have an appendix is if you get appendicitis. Appendicitis is quite common— about two people in your class will have it at some point in their lives. It means your appendix has got blocked and infected—this causes bad pain around your belly button or the lower right corner of your abdomen. Appendicitis is serious and means you need to have an operation to remove your appendix (you won't miss it, like I said—it doesn't do anything) and after that you'll be totally fine. Plus you'll have a small scar to show off. You can always claim you were attacked by a wild panther.

RECTUM — This is the last part of your large intestine, and it's a storage unit. Not for important paperwork, valuable jewelry, or wonderful memories, but for . . . you guessed it, poop. The rectum's walls expand, depending on the amount of poop that's there, and send off a signal to your brain as soon as it's time to head to the bathroom. When you're sitting comfortably, the poop makes the final part of its journey through your anus, which is the fancy word for your butthole. Well, I say it's the fancy word—you probably shouldn't say either of those words if you're having dinner with the president. To stop poop from just falling out of you while you're out shopping or playing football, your anus has some muscles in a ring shape to keep things in until it's time for . . . *Splash!* Wipe. Flush. Done. And on with your day.

POOP

Six years I trained at medical school, you know. And here I am, writing a chapter about poop. Or feces, if you'd rather use the scientific term. My parents must be so proud of me. . . . But it's an important fact of life. We all poop—film stars, singers, teachers, my dog (so, *so* often . . . where's it all coming from?)—and it's absolutely nothing to be embarrassed about. I'm not denying it's strange. Every day we sit on a specially designed piece

You might wonder why your poop is brown when you weren't eating brown food. Well, next time you're painting, try smushing all the colors together—you'll see you end up with brown. Added to that, the bile that comes out of your gallbladder makes the color darker. In fact, having light-colored poop is a sign that there might be a problem with the liver or the gallbladder stopping the bile from coming through.

of porcelain furniture and squeeze stuff out of ourselves, making all kinds of weird and not-so-wonderful sounds and smells, but it's the most natural thing in the world. Besides, it has to come out of you. There's no option— otherwise you'd end up totally full of poop, and eventually there would be an extremely messy explosion. Luckily, no one is actually full of poop, whatever the grown-ups in your life might shout at politicians on the TV.

Besides containing waste products from the food you ate, your poop has a lot of water in it—in fact, poop is mostly made of water. Even the driest, hardest poop you've ever done was more than 50 percent water. The other surprising thing about your poop is that it's alive! Don't panic—it isn't going to speak to you or fly around the room and splat you in the face. But it's still alive, thanks to hundreds of billions of bacteria. There's no need to worry, though, because these are the good bacteria that helped you digest your food. And how do we reward these good bacteria for their brilliant work? We flush them down the toilet. So disrespectful.

YOUR BUTT IS REALLY SPOTTY.

DIARRHEA

Diarrhea means that your poop isn't hard. This is ironic because the word diarrhea is *extremely* hard. In fact, if it weren't for autocorrect, I don't think I would ever spell it right. What's with that extra r? Anyway, if your poop is liquidy and it's coming more often than usual, it means that something's gotten in the way of your normal poop-producing process and your large intestine isn't absorbing water like it should. It could be because you've caught a bug, or maybe you've eaten something that has upset your insides, or it could be a side effect of some medicine you've taken. Normally diarrhea settles down on its own, but you'll need to drink plenty of fluids to replace all the water that your butt is squirting out the other end.

CONSTIPATION

Constipation is the opposite of diarrhea, and means that you're not pooping as often as normal. Everyone's "normal" is different—some people go twice a day, and some people go twice a week—but constipation means that things have slowed down in the toilet department.

There are lots of reasons why this happens, such as not drinking enough water, not eating enough vegetables (see, I *told* you they were important), or even not getting enough exercise. For some people, it's because they didn't go to the bathroom when they needed to—for example, if they were embarrassed to go at school or in a public bathroom. Never ignore your body. If it's telling you to poop, then you need to poop. (Correction: if your body tells you to cover yourself in chocolate icing, then sit in the fridge and sing Christmas carols, you should probably ignore it.)

POOP!

I DON'T FEEL LIKE IT.

IRRITABLE BOWEL SYNDROME

Irritable bowel syndrome, or IBS, means that the muscles in your gut are misbehaving. Sometimes they move too fast, causing diarrhea, and sometimes they move too slowly, causing constipation. And sometimes they alternate between the two, like a miserable seesaw of symptoms. As if that wasn't enough, IBS can also give you a stomachache and make you feel bloated, like your bowels have turned into balloons. It's very common, so if you have IBS, then your butt is in excellent company (although your doctor might want to check that it's nothing more serious). There might be certain foods that trigger your IBS, and avoiding these will mean that the symptoms improve (hopefully it's something horrible that triggers it, like mushrooms). Stress can be another cause of symptoms. The brain and the gut are very closely linked—that's why you get that fluttery feeling when you're nervous, known as butterflies in the stomach. Obviously there aren't any butterflies in there. (They're actually bats.) (Not really.)

Some people have problems with their digestive system that means they can't digest certain types of food. **LACTOSE INTOLERANCE** means your body doesn't make the enzyme that digests cow's milk, so drinking it can cause diarrhea and stomach pain. One oat milk cappuccino please! Another condition is called **CELIAC DISEASE**, which means the small intestine can't digest a substance called gluten, and eating it will also cause pain and diarrhea. It's managed by not eating anything with gluten in it, such as bread, pasta, and cakes. Relax—your cake-eating days aren't over! Nice deep breaths . . . That's better. There are gluten-free alternatives for almost anything that people with celiac disease can't eat. Celiac disease mustn't be confused with silly yak disease, which is a personality disorder affecting yaks.

The longest fart ever recorded lasted for nearly three minutes. I'm glad I wasn't trapped in an elevator with that person. It turns out farts have always been funny. The oldest joke ever discovered comes from four thousand years ago and goes like this: "Here's something that has never happened before: a woman didn't fart in her husband's lap." Hmm . . . it's not great. Maybe it lost something in translation from the ancient Sumerian.

FARTING

Doctors don't say farts—we say "flatus."

Well, we say that at work. All the rest of the time, we say "farts" like everybody else. Farts are the body's way of getting rid of any gas that's in your digestive system. Do you know why you don't mind the smell of your own farts, but everyone else's farts are vomit central? Neither do I—you can't expect me to know everything.

But I do know how gas gets into your guts: you swallow air any time you eat, and even when you talk. Various things increase the amount of air you swallow, such as drinking fizzy drinks, eating too quickly, and sucking on pens. Some of it might come out as burps, but the rest of the air will continue on its journey south. Adding to the amount of butt gas are those bacteria that live in your gut. As they feast on the food in your intestine, they produce some pretty stinky air. I'm sure you've noticed that some foods make you fart a lot more (and a lot stinkier). Beans, chickpeas, cabbage, sprouts, onions and meat all contain chemicals that cause a particularly noxious cloud to *pffffffft* out of your butt.

How often do *you* fart? Most people do it at least ten times a day. If I'm ever talking to friends and I stink the room up, I always blame it on Pippin. (I hope my friends aren't reading this. Or Pippin.)

VOMIT

We've all been there—kneeling in front of the toilet, yawning out all the colors of the rainbow. It might feel like your stomach has taken on a life of its own and is trying to escape through your mouth, but there's actually a reason for being sick: it means your body is urgently trying to get rid of something. If your stomach detects anything that shouldn't be in there—for example, food that's covered in germs—it tells your brain to activate the ejector seat. Your stomach then closes up at the bottom so food can't travel any deeper inside, your diaphragm pushes up, and your abs squeeze in. And then suddenly your lunch is all over your sweater. Oops.

The horrible smell of vomit is caused by a chemical called butyric acid. It's formed when your stomach acid breaks down food, and it smells pretty rank. Obviously we'd never deliberately eat butyric acid, right? Wrong! Butyric acid is what gives a lot of cheeses their trademark stink, so if you've ever thought that some parmesan smelled like puke, then you were quite right!

Maybe you shouldn't have eaten that week-old piece of chicken you found in the trash after all. At the same time, your mouth produces a lot more saliva to protect the enamel on your teeth, which can get damaged by the acid in your puke. You might also find yourself in a bit of a cold sweat—this is just your body trying to get rid of the heat that you've produced from this unexpected bit of exercise.

Other things can make your brain put your stomach in reverse, such as bad headaches, certain medicines, and dizziness—that's why there's a dried-up puddle of vomit at the exit of every roller coaster. What comes out of you very much depends on what you put in—strawberries and ice cream going in means strawberries and ice cream coming out (although a bit mushed up and dissolved in acid). If you're vomiting because you have a stomach bug, the puke-fest usually lasts for a day or so, even when your stomach is empty. After you've been sick, don't attempt to eat or drink anything more adventurous than sips of water to start with—otherwise it may well reappear out your mouth very soon. Right, that's enough vomit talk for one day. Let's have a breath mint and move on.

DIABETES

Besides producing enzymes to help you digest food, your pancreas has a side hustle in regulating the sugar levels in your body. It does this by producing insulin, which is a hormone that removes sugar from your blood and gives it to cells that need it. As you know, not everything in the body always goes 100 percent to plan. Sometimes your pancreas stops making insulin, and this causes the levels of sugar in your blood to shoot up. Any idea what this is called? Here's a clue: the title of this section is "diabetes." That's right! Diabetes. It can make you feel unwell, pee a lot, and have to drink loads of water, and it's something that needs to be taken care of quickly.

There are two types of diabetes, called type 1 and type 2. I do hope Clive didn't win a Nobel Prize for naming them.

TYPE 1 DIABETES — This is the most common form of diabetes in children, and it happens because your body has attacked the cells in your pancreas, for reasons we don't totally understand. Whatever the cause of this bust-up, someone with type 1 diabetes doesn't produce any insulin, and it's very important that it get replaced.

This either involves little injections or a tiny pump that continually puts insulin into the body. People with diabetes need to check their blood sugar levels regularly in case they have to increase or decrease their insulin dose. They do this either by squeezing a tiny drop of blood from a finger prick onto a little machine or by having a tiny sensor implanted under their skin. They also need to have an especially healthy diet, exercise regularly, and sometimes eat an emergency cookie if their blood sugar drops too low. People you know with diabetes are no different from you, and there's nothing you can do that they can't. (Well, except for make insulin.)

TYPE 2 DIABETES — This is a different type of diabetes that develops over time, where the pancreas usually still manages to produce a bit of insulin. It can sometimes improve with exercise and a healthier diet, and sometimes it needs to be treated with medicine. It's important to keep blood sugar levels under control, because otherwise it can affect various parts of the body—for example, the kidneys, blood vessels, and eyes. Type 2 diabetes can run in families, and often affects people who are overweight because being overweight changes how your body deals with insulin.

HEALTHY EATING

If you've ever been bored enough to read the nutritional information label on a sandwich, you'll know that food is divided into various groups. Eating the right amount of each type of food is known as having a balanced diet. Eating lunch while riding a unicycle is called an unbalanced diet, and this can result in you dropping your chips on the floor. A balanced diet means your body is getting all the fuel it needs to go about its business, so it's less likely to interrupt your busy schedule to tell you it has to see a doctor.

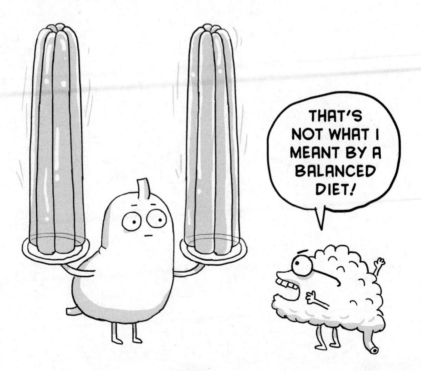

THAT'S NOT WHAT I MEANT BY A BALANCED DIET!

FRUIT AND VEGETABLES

DAIRY

CARBOHYDRATES — Want some pasta, mixed with risotto, served on a pizza base, with a slice of toast and a roast potato? No? Well, my new recipe book won't sell very well, then. You might already know that these are types of carbohydrates. Other carbs (to use their nickname) include fruit, vegetables, sugar, and honey. You don't need me to tell you that a slice of whole grain bread is better for you than a slice of cake, or that a piece of mango is better for you than a piece of chocolate. But if you did need me to tell you that, then I've just done it. There's nothing wrong with having treats, but they're things to eat in small amounts. Swap them for fruit and vegetables, which are stuffed full of vitamins and contain fiber, which stops you from getting constipated.

PROTEIN — This is what your body uses to keep its muscles healthy so you can walk and run and climb up the outside of skyscrapers. Examples of proteins include meat, fish, eggs, dairy, and wrapping paper (one of these is a slight lie). Vegans, who don't eat any animal products, can get their protein from soy, tofu, beans, and lentils. Too much red meat (such as steak) is bad for you, so it's better to stick to lighter meat like chicken or fish.

FAT — A small amount of fat is important as part of a healthy diet: your body needs fat to make new cells. Some kinds of fat (called unsaturated fats) are actually very good for you and hang around in things like fish, nuts, and avocados. Basically, the next time you eat a salmon stuffed with avocado and peanuts, then you'll be eating a lot of unsaturated fats. Saturated fats, on the other hand, are bad for you if you have too much of them. They live in things like cookies (sorry), cakes (really sorry), pies (sorry again), sausages (I said I'm sorry), and fried mushrooms (okay, those can go in the trash). Eating too much saturated fat for too long causes issues with your health—in particular, it can gunk up your blood vessels and make it harder for your heart to pump.

VITAMINS

Vitamins are tiny little parts of food that help your body do all the things it needs to. If you eat lots of different types of food, including plenty of fruits, nuts, seeds, vegetables, and pigeon beaks, then it's likely you'll get all the vitamins you need. (Actually, you don't need to eat pigeon beaks—ignore that part.) Some people need to take vitamins to boost things they're missing, especially if there are foods they can't eat for medical reasons, or sometimes if they're vegetarian or vegan. Even though vitamins are important, it's possible to take too much of some of them, so you shouldn't take vitamins unless you're advised to. For example, too much vitamin A can be dangerous, and some people have even died from it.

VITAMIN A — Helps you fight off illness and makes it easier to see in the dark—no, seriously. It lurks in milk, cheese, eggs, and fish.

VITAMIN B — Vitamin B is like a spider with eight separate legs. Oops, I've made it sound terrifying. What I'm saying is there are eight different types of vitamin B, with jobs ranging from keeping your nerves healthy, helping your skin, releasing energy from the food you eat, and making red blood cells. If that's the sort of stuff that's important to you (clue: it is), then make sure you eat things like eggs, green vegetables, milk, fish, and meat. Although maybe not all at once in a horrendous sandwich.

VITAMIN C — This helps your wounds heal and keeps your skin, blood vessels and bones healthy. It's found in lots of types of fruits and vegetables, especially in colorful foods like oranges, peppers, and strawberries (but sadly not Haribo). A lack of vitamin C is called scurvy, and it used to happen to sailors who couldn't get any fresh food on their long trips at sea.

Given the farthest you've been from dry land was probably lying on an inflatable unicorn in a hotel swimming pool, you've got no excuse.

VITAMIN D — Vitamin D thinks hanging out in food is a bit boring, so it prefers to come at you via sunlight. There are some foods that contain it too, such as eggs, fish, and certain kinds of meat. It's there to keep your bones, muscles, and teeth strong. Very handy if you need to wrestle a woolly mammoth (and then eat it).

VITAMIN E — Yet another thing that keeps your immune system healthy, plus it helps your skin and eyes. It's found in cereals, nuts, seeds, and green vegetables. (Vitamins are always found in stuff like this, I'm afraid, rather than bags of sweets and double-decker pizzas.)

VITAMIN K — Nope, I've got no idea what happened to vitamins F, G, H, I, and J—maybe the inventor of vitamins didn't learn the alphabet correctly? (I might just make something up. Vitamin F is in frogs, vitamin G is in ghosts, vitamin H is in hockey pucks, vitamin I is in icebergs, and vitamin J is in jellyfish.) Vitamin K helps your blood clot—without it, your knee would still be bleeding from when you fell over three weeks ago. It's found in milk, meat, and green vegetables (those guys again).

MINERALS — You'll be pleased to hear there's no need to suck on pebbles, but there are a few minerals your body needs in addition to its shopping list of vitamins. For example, calcium helps your bones and muscles, and you get it from dairy foods and green vegetables. You also need iron, for making red blood cells, and you'll find plenty of it in meat, beans, nuts, and rice (even though they don't look very shiny).

BODY SIZE

If we eat more food than our bodies need to use for fuel, any excess gets stored under the skin and around the organs as body fat. Some of us burn off fuel more easily than others—the speed this happens at is known as your metabolism, and it's something else to blame (or thank) your biological parents for.

Besides keeping your body healthy, it's just as important to keep your mind healthy—this means not focusing too much on your weight or on how you look, or comparing yourself to others. People can become very unhappy and even unwell when they spend lots of time thinking about what they eat. They often think they look much bigger than they actually are, and can develop eating disorders such as anorexia and bulimia.

ANOREXIA — People with anorexia eat very little food, and sometimes exercise far too much, so that they lose weight.

BULIMIA — People with bulimia eat large amounts of food in one go (this is called binge eating), then make themselves vomit or take medicines that make them poop it straight out.

These are both very serious conditions that can cause major health problems. It's really important to speak to an adult if you think you might have an eating disorder so you can get help with it.

Whatever you look like—whether you're big or small, short or tall, have one leg or two, lots of hair or none— you're beautiful and brilliant and you must always remember that. I can guarantee you that every single person who you admire or think is perfect had a huge list of things they wanted to change about themselves at some point—and maybe they still do. You only have one body and one life, and it's important to celebrate your body for what it is, and to have fun. Speaking of which, I'd better get back to building my electronic fart machine.

KAY'S ZWESTIONS

WHY DOES MY STOMACH RUMBLE WHEN I'M HUNGRY?

You're actually hearing your intestines rather than your stomach. As you know, the muscles in your intestines are constantly moving and pushing

Disaster! The computer shop ordered a Z key by accident.

things buttward. They make noise all the time, but when there's food inside them it muffles the sound—if you stuffed a trumpet full of chips and yogurt it wouldn't be very loud. (If you try this, don't tell your parents it was me who suggested it.) When your intestines are empty, you can hear the rumbling in its full gurgling glory. Those rumbles have a medical name: borborygmus. See if your science teacher knows that. . . . If not, you should probably seize control of the class and declare yourself the new teacher.

WHY DO I FART MORE ON PLANES?

Nope, it has nothing to do with airplane food. In the sky, planes have a lower air pressure than on dry land, and this means that the gas in your intestines expands. More gas in your intestines means—you guessed it—more farts. Remember to apologize to the people sitting behind you . . . or alternatively, blame it on them?

WHY DOESN'T STOMACH ACID DISSOLVE THE WALL OF MY STOMACH?

Good point. This acid is so strong that it can even dissolve metal, so you'd think it would make very quick work of a bit of stomach. Luckily, your stomach produces some thick mucus to protect itself and stop you from eating yourself from the inside. (Please don't eat yourself from the outside either.)

TRUE OR POO?

YOUR FIRST POOP WAS DARK GREEN.

TRUE Your first poop as a baby was goopy, gross, and green. When you're born, your guts have got a load of junk in them, such as mucus, bile, and a bunch of old cells. Better hope your parents didn't put your first poop on Instagram—it's not your finest work.

YOU NEED YOUR LARGE INTESTINE TO LIVE.

POO At least 500,000 people in the United States have had surgery to remove part of their intestines—that's five times as many people as would fit in Wembley Stadium. It's often because they had cancer, or it could be because of conditions that caused the wall of their intestines to become very red and swollen, like Crohn's disease or ulcerative colitis. (Most people with these illnesses don't need to have operations—they just take medicine.) If you don't have a large intestine, then you can still lead the life you want. The only difference is that instead of coming out of the usual place, the poop goes into a bag at the bottom of your abdomen.

EATING BEETS MAKES YOUR POOP TURN PURPLE.

TRUE Too many beets and your poop suddenly becomes a lot more exotic than its usual sludgy brown color. If you forgot that you ate beets earlier, then you might worry that your poop has been possessed by an alien.

If you have red or purple colors in your poop and you don't know why, it's important to ask an adult, because blood in your poop can mean there's something wrong.

CHAPTER 11
KIDNEYS AND LIVER

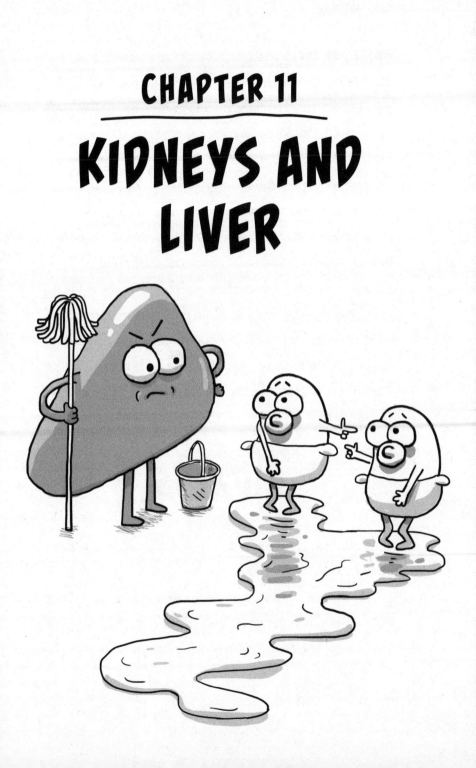

WASTE PRODUCTS are just a fact of life—there's always stuff that needs to be chucked out. The packaging that you put in the recycling, the orange peel that gets composted, the empty yogurt cup that you throw at your brother. And . . . your pee.

Pee (or urine, to use its formal name) is *so* much more than yellowy water that tinkles out of you every few hours. It literally saves your life every single day. Honestly, it does—by clearing poisonous waste products from your bloodstream. It might end up down the toilet, or at the side of the road if you forgot to go at the last rest stop, or squirted up the side of a tree if you're Pippin, but it takes quite a journey through your body to get there.

KIDNEYS

You have two kidneys (well, some of you might only have one, actually); they live at the back of your body under your ribs, and they're about the size of your fist. Your right kidney is lower down than the left one because the liver's a bit of a bully and pushes it out of the way.

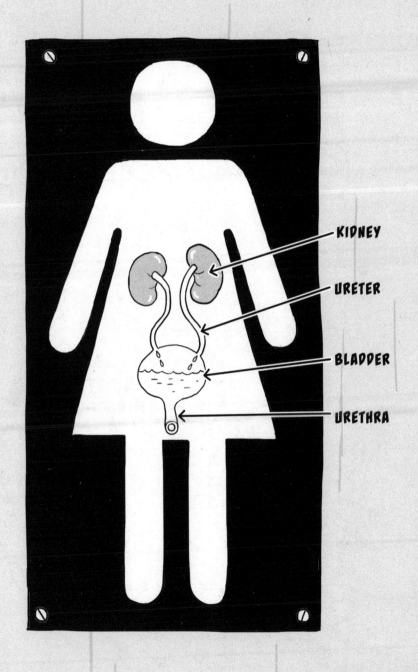

KIDNEY

URETER

BLADDER

URETHRA

Kidneys are shaped like a type of bean. Which one is it again? It's not a chickpea. . . . It's not a lentil. . . . Pretty sure it's not a black bean. . . . Dunno, maybe I'll remember later. Your kidneys' mission in life is to get waste out of your blood. Your kidneys are a bit like bouncers, deciding what's allowed to stay in the blood and what needs to be kicked out.

When I say waste, I don't mean rotten turnips and moldy old sneakers, I mean stuff that the cells of your body have used up, and excess nutrients that they don't need. The kidney cells (known as nephrons, just to make your life a bit more complicated) are a million minuscule water filters, which make this happen.

Another thing the kidneys do is make sure that your body has the right amount of water in it. If you don't have enough water in your blood (known as dehydration), then that's bad for you, but so is having too much water. . . . What a nightmare! Luckily, your kidneys are on hand to keep everything nicely balanced. If there's too much water in your body and you're in danger of puffing up like a big blimp, the kidneys remove water from your blood. But if you're dehydrated, the kidneys only take a tiny amount so you don't shrivel up like a sun-dried tomato. If you've wondered why your pee is sometimes totally clear and sometimes dark yellow, it's all to do with how much water is in your system. (If it's dark yellow, drink more water. Doctor's orders.)

Every day, your kidneys make about a liter and a half of urine—enough to fill one of those big bottles of lemonade. Maybe you should have a sniff before you pour yourself a glass of lemonade next time, in case someone has been testing this theory out.

Once the pee is ready for transportation, it whizzes down a waterslide called the ureter. You have two ureters—one for each kidney—and they're about as long as a school ruler. (But thinner. And not made out of plastic. And they don't go *BOIIIIIING!* when you twang them on your desk.) The ureters connect to your bladder, which is a bag of muscle that stores your pee, like the world's worst swimming pool.

POOL RULES:

NO RUNNING.
NO DIVING.
PEEING
COMPULSORY.

Your kidneys are constantly making urine and sending a trickle of it down to your bladder. (Or, to put it another way, you are peeing yourself internally all day long.) The bladder is important because it holds on to the pee until you're ready to go to the toilet, and stretches in size to store it. Once it has stretched to the size of a grapefruit, your bladder sends a message to your brain telling you it's time to go to the bathroom—I'm sure you know that feeling. Your pee then has one last bit of the journey to make before it escapes to the outside world. The muscle at the bottom of your bladder opens, and the pee travels down a final tube called the urethra. If you want to know a bit more about the yellow stuff, then *urine* luck. (Sorry.)

A lot of the water that goes into our bodies actually comes from food rather than drink. You might already know that tomatoes and cucumbers are about 95 percent water, but even bread is mostly made of water. Mmmm . . . Imagine drinking a refreshing cup of bread on a hot day.

URINE

Pee is mostly plain old water, but it gets its attractive yellow color from blood cells that have gone into retirement and been smushed up by your body. It contains lots of salt, but please don't pee on your fries (or mine, more importantly), and there's also a substance called urea in it, which is formed from all those waste products I was telling you about before. Your pee doesn't smell particularly strong when it's fresh out of your body, but you might have noticed that public toilets don't always smell great. . . . This is because if urine is left to hang around for too long, bacteria munch away on the urea (hey, we've all got to eat!) and cause that familiar odor.

Have you ever wondered why doctors are so interested in taking samples of your pee? Are they collecting it all for some kind of hideous museum? Well, possibly— I don't know about your doctor's hobbies.

But also, urine can tell doctors a lot about what's going on inside you. For example, it can show if you have too much sugar in your blood, which could be a sign of diabetes. These days, doctors test urine using special kits or send it off to a lab, but in the olden days they had a much more basic way of telling how much sugar was in there. Yep, they tasted it. I'm glad I didn't work as a doctor back then. Urine tests can also see if you have a urine infection, which can cause abdominal pain, frequent peeing, and painful peeing. Not much fun, but easily treated with antibiotics.

LIVING WITH ONE KIDNEY

Lots of people are born with one kidney, and this generally doesn't cause any issues—but it's especially important for them to look after their lone kidney, because they don't have a spare! People with one kidney are often advised to avoid sports such as boxing, hockey, and football, where it could get injured.

There is a condition called kidney stones where adults form—you guessed it—stones inside their kidneys. This can be very painful and cause blood in the urine, which is always a reason to speak to a doctor. Most people only get one or two kidney stones at once, but the world record for the number of kidney stones removed was over 170,000— enough to gravel an entire driveway.

There are also some people who were born with two kidneys but decided to give one of them away. This is usually because a relative of theirs has severe kidney problems, and they donated a kidney so that relative can live longer. It's an amazingly kind thing to do—probably the single kindest thing a person can ever do. My friend Emma gave her dad a kidney. (I once gave my dad a Twix—also kind, but not quite the same.)

LIVER

Right, I think we've spent enough time wading around in pee. It's time to turn our attention to the liver. The liver loiters in the right-hand side of your tummy, tucked under your rib cage. It's bigger than the brain, it's shaped like a massive wedge of cheese, it's kind of reddish brown, and if you could touch it, it would feel rubbery. (I strongly recommend you not touch it.) Like a lot of organs, the liver is divided into lobes, but just to mix things up a bit, the liver's four lobes are each divided into tiny little lobules. Cute! (Ignore that— I've just looked at a liver lobule and they're not cute at all.)

Your liver is a bit of an overachiever, and it does *a lot* of jobs—it has a to-do list longer than an unfurled roll of toilet paper. Seriously, it has at least five hundred different functions. And now I'm going to tell you about every single one of them. (Or maybe just the main three.)

CLEANING — First up is removing poisons from food. Even though you didn't have arsenic soup for lunch (I hope), a lot of things become poisonous once your digestive system has taken the good stuff out of them— and then it's up to your liver to boot them out.

STORING FUEL — Your body is very good at storing excess energy from food that it doesn't need to use—that's what fat is—but the liver also helps out by storing glucose (a type of sugar). If you haven't eaten for a while, or if you're doing some exercise, then your liver can rush some sugar straight into your bloodstream. What a service.

MAKING BILE — Another one of your liver's many talents is making bile. You heard about it in the last chapter—your liver is always making it, storing it in a handy little bag called the gallbladder, then finally squirting it into your intestines to help you digest food. You've probably also seen bile before—it's the yellowy-green liquid that sometimes comes up when you're getting sick, after everything else in your stomach has already landed on the carpet. (Sorry to remind you of unhappier, pukier times.) Bile is also one of the things that gives your poop its trademark brown color. Wow, puke and poop in one paragraph—is that some kind of record? Next time, I'll try to fit in pee and snot too.

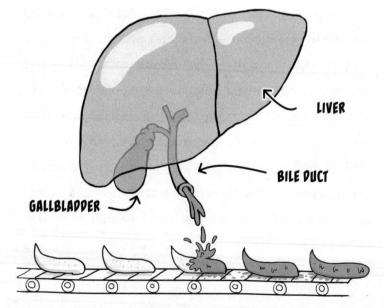

LIVER

BILE DUCT

GALLBLADDER

Your liver can completely regenerate! Is it an alien? (Probably not.) But because it's such an important organ, it has an extra way to protect itself—even if half of its cells are destroyed, it can simply grow back, in a matter of weeks. Can you imagine if all your body worked that way? "Oh, my arm's fallen off! No worries. It'll grow back next week!" (Spoiler alert: it won't, so please don't chop anything off.)

ALCOHOL

Even though your liver has Wolverine-like regeneration abilities, it has its limits, and can still suffer permanent damage, or even stop working entirely. A very common reason for liver failure is drinking alcohol. This is a bit confusing because there are bars everywhere and alcohol is for sale in supermarkets— but, like cigarettes and unhealthy foods, just because it's legal doesn't mean you can have as much as you like. The government tells us the maximum amount of alcohol to drink each week to avoid serious health problems, but despite this some people drink more than the recommended limit and cause themselves harm. Alcohol is addictive, which means it can be very hard to stop once you've started using it. While you're growing up, any amount of alcohol is bad for you—it doesn't just affect the liver, it also damages the brain and bones. And you need those to work, assuming you enjoy doing things like walking, thinking, and talking.

People become "drunk" because the liver is a bit slow at processing alcohol. (I don't mean to criticize livers—I'm just telling the truth.) It takes about an hour for the liver to remove a small alcoholic drink from your bloodstream. Until then, the alcohol sloshes around, affecting your vision, your hearing, and your steadiness. It can also affect your decision-making and cause you to do unsafe things and feel out of control—lots of accidents happen to people when they've had alcohol. This is why it's totally illegal and really dangerous to drive a car when you're drunk.

The more drinks someone has, the longer it takes for the liver to get rid of the alcohol. Think how easy it would be for you to hit a tennis ball if one was served at you every twenty seconds. Simple—you've got this. But what if tennis balls started coming at you every single second? You'd only be able to hit some of them back—the rest would just whizz past you. That's what happens if you drink too much too quickly—the liver just can't cope. This is called "binge drinking," and it's extremely bad for your liver.

Doctors and nurses in hospitals have enough work to do without people making their lives harder by drinking too much alcohol. As if alcohol doesn't cause enough problems already, the morning after drinking you get something called a hangover. It makes you feel like you've been hit on the head with a baseball bat, and it's partly caused by dehydration and partly because of the poisons still swirling around your body.

THIS IS HOW HENRY DRAWS WHEN HE'S DRUNK ALCOHOL.

I'm not going to tell you to never drink alcohol. Most people who drink alcohol have a small amount every so often, enjoy it, and live very healthy lives. But I am going to tell you four things.

1. Please don't even think about drinking alcohol until you're older. It can cause long-term damage, and nothing's worth that. If your friends are drinking alcohol (because they haven't read this book), then it's absolutely fine to say you don't want any.

2. When you're older, always keep an eye on how much you're drinking. The health guidelines are there for a reason, and they're an upper limit, not an aim. No one wants to be on the waiting list for a liver transplant, wishing they'd drunk less over the years.

3. People are very, very boring when they're drunk, and they have terrible breath.

4. Alcohol is expensive—there are lots of other things you can spend your money on that you don't just pee out a few hours later!

KAY'S KWESTIONS

WHY DO SOME PEOPLE WET THE BED?

There are lots of reasons why this can happen, and none of them are anything to be embarrassed about. The body is strange and complicated, and not everything always works exactly as it should. Your bladder might only be able to hold a small amount of pee in it, or you might be a really deep sleeper and miss the signals from your brain telling you to wake up and pop to the bathroom. If this is the case, then you should go before bedtime, and not drink anything for an hour or so beforehand—especially not fizzy drinks or drinks with caffeine in them. It can also be a sign that you're stressed about something. It will absolutely stop happening, but sometimes it's worth getting checked out by a doctor in case something unusual is causing it, like an infection in the urine or diabetes.

Okay, they've finally ordered the right key. I'll be spelling that word correctly any time now.

HOW MUCH WATER SHOULD I DRINK IN A DAY?

It depends on lots of things, like your age, whether you're male or a female, and whether or not you run a marathon in the Sahara Desert every afternoon. On average, it's around one and a half liters, which is about five big glasses of water. It's better to drink too much water than too little—your kidneys can always do their famous "water into pee" routine.

WHY DOES STEAM COME OFF MY PEE?

Simple—there's a tiny kettle in your bladder. I might have gotten that a little bit wrong, actually—it's not steam you're seeing, it's water vapor. Your pee is the same temperature as your body, which you'll hopefully remember is 98.6 degrees. If you didn't remember, go and sit in a bath of slugs as a punishment. This is a lot hotter than most rooms (unless you live on top of a volcano), so when you pee some of the water in it turns into vapor.

TRUE OR POO?

IN A SURVIVAL SITUATION, DRINKING YOUR PEE CAN HELP YOU STAY ALIVE.

TRUE It's very important to mention that this is for emergencies only. If you want to drink something more interesting than water, may I suggest a glass of milk rather than going straight for the yellow stuff. You sometimes hear of people trapped in awful situations who manage to stay alive by drinking their own pee, and this is because it's mostly made of water. But your pee has quite a lot of bad stuff in there too (that's the whole point of it—to get the nasties out), so putting it back into your body isn't a great idea. If you were to drink it for more than a day or two, you'd definitely start doing more harm than good.

PEEING ON A JELLYFISH STING HELPS WITH THE PAIN.

POO I'm glad this isn't true, aren't you? I think I'd rather take my chances with a jellyfish than be peed on. I'm not quite sure how this rumor started, but urine can actually cause the pain to get worse rather than better. In which case, you're not only in more agony, but you're also covered in someone else's pee.

YOU HAVE DRUNK YOUR OWN PEE BEFORE.

TRUE Sorry, but you have. In fact, it's all you drank nonstop for months. No, it wasn't that school milk that tasted a bit weird—it was while you were a baby, growing in the uterus. Before they're born, babies drink the fluid that they float in, but—plot twist—that fluid also contains what the babies pee out. So you didn't just swallow pee, you also swam in it. Sorry to break the news to you like this.

CHAPTER 12
REPRODUCTION

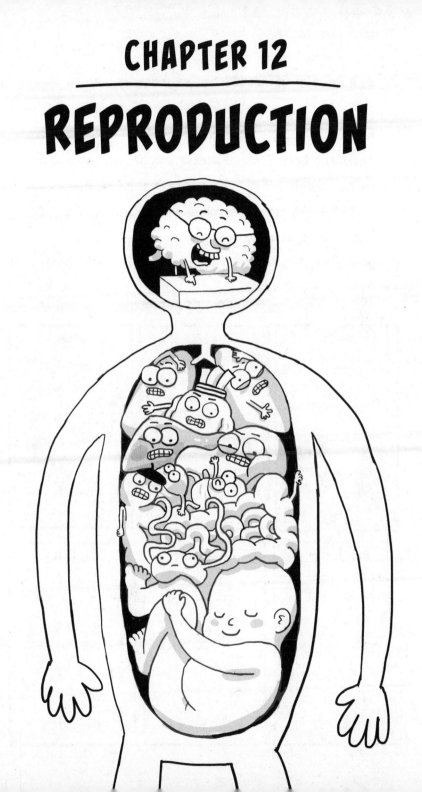

HOW DID YOU GET HERE? I don't mean right here, right now—like sitting on your bed, or on a bench, or on the International Space Station (astronauts need to learn about the body too). Of course you know how you got *there*. I mean, how you got here in the first place. You might have heard a few explanations in the past, involving some birds and some bees (nope), a stork (nope again), or growing from a type of seed (closer . . . but still nope).

HOW YOU DIDN'T GET HERE

All living things can reproduce, which means they can have children. (Who'd want children? Yuck! Oh, sorry, I apologize— I forgot you're a child. Ignore that.) It's what makes us different from nonliving things like steering wheels, cutlery, and candlesticks (unless you've got creepy talking candlesticks, like in *Beauty and the Beast*).

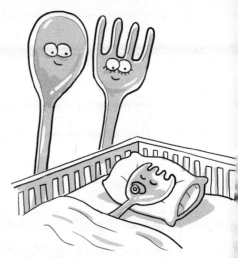

Different living things reproduce in different ways. For example, bacteria produce identical clones of themselves every twenty minutes. It's just as well that doesn't happen to humans; otherwise you'd have to share your bedroom with another ten thousand of you, which would be extremely crowded (and wouldn't smell great either). And strawberry plants develop baby plants at the ends of their roots. I'm glad humans don't do that either, because it would be pretty scary if we started sprouting tiny humans at the bottom of our legs.

All mammals, whether they're horses, hippos, hares, hedgehogs, or humans, have babies using a process

The reproductive system
is one of the only organs that we don't
rely on to stay alive. It creates life, sure—but,
unlike your brain or heart or liver or kidneys,
if your reproductive system doesn't work, you
can still lead your life as usual.

called sexual

reproduction, which

involves a bit of specialist equipment known as

the reproductive system. Want to know more? Read on.

Couldn't care less? How rude. (I take back my earlier

apology.)

THE REPRODUCTIVE SYSTEM

The reproductive system is the stuff that lives in your
underwear, plus some other bits of machinery hidden
inside your body. What you call these parts may vary,
and there are lots of strange/funny/appalling slang
names for them, but if you're going to give something a
nickname you should probably be familiar with it first.
(Pippin's nickname is Pip, or Weaselface if she's just
eaten my dinner when I wasn't looking.)

I guess you might have noticed that male and female
bodies look different, and it's the reproductive systems
that are the most different parts of all. But even though

they look different, they both have the same job: to make and store a special ingredient needed for reproduction. For males the ingredient in question is the sperm, and for females it's the egg, also known as the ovum. (Ovum is the Latin word for egg—handy knowledge if you ever find yourself ordering breakfast in ancient Rome. I recommend the scrambled ovum and a Caesar salad.) Separately, the sperm and the egg don't do very much, but when they meet, the sperm fertilizes the egg, which means they begin to form a baby. It's like the world's easiest jigsaw, with only two pieces.

FEMALE REPRODUCTIVE SYSTEM

The part of the female reproductive system that's visible on the outside is called the vulva. You might call it another name yourself, and in the playground you might have heard some of those less science-y names I mentioned, but this is its proper, medical name. The vulva has small flaps of skin at the side called the labia, and everyone's looks different— it's a unique part of you. Inside the vulva is a little nub called the clitoris and two openings: the urethra (which you'll remember is the tube that carries pee out from the bladder) and the vagina.

Kangaroos have three vaginas. Probably not a fact you'll ever need to know in your entire life, but there you go.

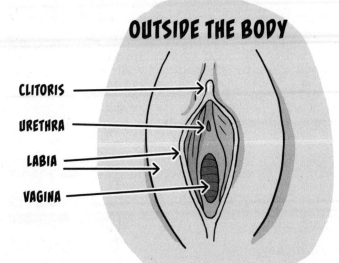

OUTSIDE THE BODY

CLITORIS

URETHRA

LABIA

VAGINA

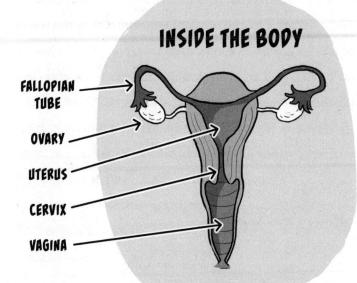

INSIDE THE BODY

FALLOPIAN TUBE

OVARY

UTERUS

CERVIX

VAGINA

The vagina is a tunnel that connects the outside of the reproductive system to the uterus (more on that soon). Most tunnels you've met before will have had solid walls that don't move, but the vagina's walls are made out of muscle, so it can get wider or narrower if it needs to— for example, if a baby is coming out through it.

Speaking of babies, the uterus is where they grow during pregnancy. The uterus is usually about the size of a plum, but if a woman is pregnant it grows to the size of, well, a baby.

Between the uterus and the vagina is the cervix. It's like a tiny rubber ring that acts as a security guard, deciding what's allowed in and out of the uterus. Up at the top of the uterus are two pipes called fallopian tubes which lead to the ovaries. The ovaries are where the eggs live and the fallopian tubes are the waterslides which the eggs zoom down once a month. When a female baby is born, her ovaries already contain all the eggs she'll ever have, but they don't really do anything until puberty—which is an *extremely* long nap, if you ask me.

MALE REPRODUCTIVE SYSTEM

One big difference between the male and female reproductive systems is that the female one is mostly on the inside, but the male one is mostly on the outside, dangling there like a chandelier. First of all, there's the penis. Insert any name you like for it there, but I'm a doctor and I say the word penis. (I don't mean I say it constantly—that would be weird and people would stop inviting me to parties.) Like the labia, every penis is a different size and shape. The end of the penis is often covered with a flap of skin called the foreskin—some people have it, and some people have had it removed, but everything works just the same with or without it.

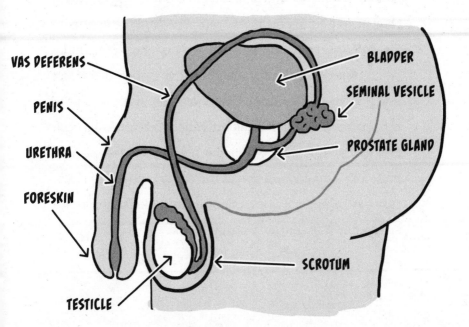

VAS DEFERENS

PENIS

URETHRA

FORESKIN

TESTICLE

BLADDER

SEMINAL VESICLE

PROSTATE GLAND

SCROTUM

Hanging there under the penis is a bag called the scrotum, and in there are the testicles, whose job is to make sperm. It might seem like a bit of a design fault to have such important things on the outside of the body, where they could get damaged, but the testicles have their reasons. A bit like famous pop stars who demand that their dressing room be filled with white lilies and bowls of M&Ms with the green ones taken out, the testicles insist on a certain temperature. They find the body's heat a bit too much for them to get on with producing sperm, so they hang around outside instead. (Fair enough, I say—it's hard to concentrate when it's too hot. Have you ever tried doing your math homework in a sauna?) Because your testicles live out in the suburbs, they need a transportation system to send the sperm on its way: little tubes called the vas deferens. (Hopefully you'll remember their name, but if you don't it doesn't make a *vast difference*.) These join the urethra to take the sperm to the outside world. (The urethra carries both pee and sperm, although never both at once—like how you can't sing and whistle at the same time.) Boys never run out of sperm: they constantly make them every single day from puberty onward.

PUBERTY

There's more to growing up than having extra candles on your birthday cake and taking up more space on the sofa. I'm talking about puberty, which means your reproductive system is about to spring into life. Like me on a Sunday, your reproductive system sits around doing nothing much for quite a long time. And then suddenly, *boom!*—it's Monday morning and it's time to get to work. Puberty can start at any time, usually at some point between the ages of eight and fourteen, with boys generally kicking off a bit later than girls. The changes happen over years and years—don't worry if things happen sooner or later, or faster or slower, for you compared with your friends. Everyone is different, but we all get there eventually.

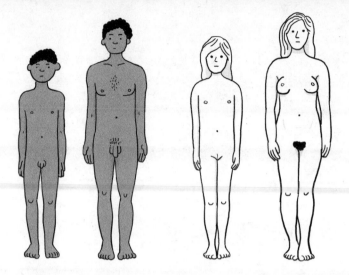

I won't lie—puberty can be a strange old time, but just remember, every single grown-up you know has been through this, and they all turned out okay. (Apart from your principal, obviously.) It all happens when certain hormones wake up—hormones are those chemical messengers that tell your body what to do, like a particularly bossy gym teacher. In boys the hormone that increases the most is called testosterone, and the head girl hormone is called estrogen.

HAIR

Puberty means that things are going to get hairy. Hair will start to appear on all sorts of different bits of your body, like under your arms and around your penis or vulva. The hair on your head might get greasier, and boys will start to grow hair on their faces, although it appears very slowly at first. In fact, you're unlikely to be able to enter the World's Most Amazing Beard competition until you're at least eighteen. Apologies, fellas.

BODY SHAPE

You might suddenly grow very fast—it can feel like you've been stretched on some kind of medieval torture device, because your arms and legs are suddenly so looooooong. Girls' bodies get curvier and their hips change shape, until they're wide enough to be able to give birth. And boys' muscles get bigger—they might not be able to spot this, but it's happening under the surface, trust me. We're not talking enough muscles to lift a car over your head, I'm afraid—just more than before.

SKIN

You know I mentioned acne in the skin chapter? (I'll wait for you to quickly reread that part now. . . . I might boil the kettle and make myself a cup of tea. Oh no, the milk carton's all ripped! Who drank all the . . . *PIPPIN!*) Well, puberty hormones are what make those pesky pimples appear on your face, and maybe also on your chest, back, and shoulders. You'll find yourself sweating more, which might make you smell not so great, while all this puberty stuff is going on. Although there's nothing you can do about most things that happen during puberty, you can keep the BO at bay by taking regular showers and using deodorant. Not too much, though, or you'll smell like an explosion in a perfume factory.

VOICE

One of the things that testosterone does is make the voice box in your neck grow, and this causes your voice to drop permanently. In boys, we call this the voice "breaking," but it's not broken, it's fine—put down the glue stick. When a boy's voice breaks, it drops by about an octave (that's eight white notes on the piano, if you fell asleep during music lessons). The front of a boy's neck sticks out a bit as the voice box grows—people call this an Adam's apple. (I just call it an apple.)

ADAM'S APPLE　　**ADAM'S BANANA**　　**ADAM'S CHEESE AND TOMATO BAGUETTE**

Girls also have testosterone, but much less of it, so their voices drop during puberty, but only by a note or two.

PENIS

As the male body develops, the penis and testicles get bigger, and the testicles prepare to make sperm. The penis will sometimes get hard, which is called an erection and means extra blood has flowed in there. Blood is always flowing to the penis (otherwise it would fall off—ouch), but there are empty spaces within it that can fill up when needed, which makes the penis swell. It can be a bit embarrassing when an erection happens when you're not expecting it, but it's the same for all boys, if that's any consolation.

BREASTS

One of the most obvious physical changes in the female body during puberty is that the breasts and nipples will grow. This process can take a few years, and the breasts can change a few times before they settle on a final shape—everyone's end up different shapes and sizes, totally unique to them. If women decide to have children, then their breasts have a job to do: they produce milk (or they lactate, if you're collecting fancy words), which provides babies with all the nutrition they need. Not everyone with a baby is able to breastfeed, or chooses to, but it's a healthy (and free!) source of baby food. Boys don't grow breasts like girls do, but things might swell a little in that area for a short while—nothing at all to worry about.

BRAIN

Besides the four million changes to your body that puberty throws your way, you might find yourself feeling different inside too. You might get annoyed more easily, or become upset for no obvious reason. You might feel tired, or anxious, or sensitive. This is because your brain is making a few changes, and just like any computer, not every software update goes smoothly.

PERIODS

Periods (or menstruation, if you prefer words with more syllables) are a big new change that happens to the female body. During puberty, the ovaries begin to release eggs about once a month. No one knows how the ovary decides which egg is going to be released that cycle, but I bet it's either a talent contest or a game of Scrabble.

If an egg is released but there's no sperm to meet it, then it doesn't get fertilized and won't grow into a baby. The lining of the uterus, where a fertilized egg would implant, goes, "Well, I guess there's nothing for me to do here," and comes out of the vagina as a small amount of blood. The lining re-forms a couple of weeks later. The most common age for periods to start is around twelve or thirteen, but they can start earlier or later than that. They usually last somewhere between a few days and a week, and even though they'll eventually happen roughly once a month, it can take a couple of years for them to settle into this pattern.

On average, the amount of blood that comes out every month would fit in an egg cup—for some people it's less than this, and for some it's more. If you're worried about the amount of bleeding, then make sure you speak to an adult about it. Girls and women use products to stop blood from getting on their clothes while they're having their period, such as pads (which sit inside their underwear), tampons (which are thin little cylinders of material that go inside the vagina), menstrual cups (little plastic-y cups that are inserted into the vagina), and period pants (underwear made with a special absorbent lining). Using these means no one can tell when you have your period, and you can get on with juggling rattlesnakes while riding a unicycle (or whatever it is you like doing). Periods can cause cramping abdominal pains, and a hot-water bottle can sometimes help with that. If period pains get really bad, then always ask an adult for help.

HUMAN REPRODUCTION

Reproduction means a man's erect penis goes into a woman's vagina and releases lots of microscopic sperm. It only takes one single sperm to fertilize the egg, but because a man produces millions and millions of them, they all have to take part in a miniature version of the Olympics. Sperm look a little bit like tadpoles, and to reach the egg they have to swim to it—up the vagina, through the cervix, into the uterus, and up a fallopian tube. The sperm that reaches the egg first is the one to fertilize it and complete the jigsaw puzzle. Phew! Sadly, there's no second, third, fourth, or millionth prize for the sperm who arrive afterward—bad luck.

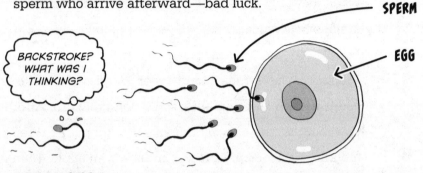

SPERM

EGG

BACKSTROKE? WHAT WAS I THINKING?

PREGNANCY

The fertilized egg now begins its fairly major job of transforming from a couple of cells into a whole baby. It doubles in size from two cells to four, then from four cells to eight, then sixteen, then thirty-two, then . . . whatever two times thirty-two is. (Hey, it's not a math book—how should I know?) This ball of cells, known as an embryo, nestles into the lining of the uterus, where it can start snacking on all the nutrients it needs to grow.

PREGNANCY is a huge old subject—I could write a whole book about it. (Please don't make me—I'm exhausted from writing this one.) But here are some highlights, like when they only show the highlight reel on ESPN instead of the whole game.

Pregnancy lasts nine months—or 280 days, if you're counting, which pregnant people definitely are. After two months, the baby is the size of a grape. At three months, it's a lemon. At four months, it's an apple. Then at five months, it's a mango. I mean, it's the size of a mango—it's obviously not an actual mango.

The pregnant body goes through a lot of changes—there's more to pregnancy than a massive bump. For example, all the mom's organs will shuffle out of the way to make room for this massive, baby-sized uterus. (That's why pregnant women often get out of breath—their lungs are squished up higher than usual.)

The amount of blood a pregnant woman has sloshing around in her veins and arteries goes from around four liters to six liters—this is because babies get all their oxygen and nutrients from their mom's blood, so she

BUNGEE!

needs to have plenty of extra. You'll be pleased to hear that babies don't drink this blood, so you didn't spend nine months as a miniature vampire. It's delivered via a big fleshy thing called the **PLACENTA**, which attaches to the baby through a tube called the **UMBILICAL CORD**. It's really important that a pregnant mom doesn't smoke or drink much alcohol, because this can badly affect how the baby develops.

After roughly nine months, it's the baby's birthday. Fingers crossed it's a good birthday in the summer, so they don't need to spend it at school every year. The pregnant mom goes into **LABOR**, which means the muscles of the uterus squeeze really tightly every couple of minutes (these are called contractions). This makes the cervix open up over a number of hours, and then finally she can push the baby out through her vagina. Some babies are born by **CESAREAN SECTION**, which is an operation on the abdomen to remove the baby by making a cut into the uterus. It's a bit like getting out of the car using the sunroof (although much less dangerous). Cesarean sections are commonly used for twins, for babies who are lying feet first in the uterus, or for babies who get stuck or distressed during labor.

And then *ta-da!* One baby. Or two, or three . . . or eight, aka octuplets, which is the world record for a single pregnancy. Well, for a single human pregnancy, anyway— the African driver ant has about four million babies every month. They must spend a fortune on babysitters.

ULTRASOUND

The very first photo of you was probably taken when you were minus half a year old. X-rays aren't safe in pregnancy, so the best way to get that snap of you is by using ultrasound. I hope you remembered to smile. Along with having a look into a pregnant abdomen, ultrasounds are also good for looking at muscles, joints, and organs like the liver and kidneys. They work by firing off sound waves that are so high you can't hear them—a bit like how bats and dolphins detect things. (Please always make sure that the person doing your ultrasound is a human, and not a bat or a dolphin.)

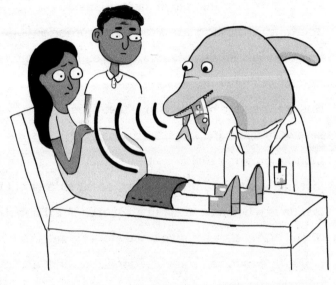

IVF

Unless you really skimmed through this chapter in a hurry, you'll have noticed that there are a lot of steps in the process of fertilization, involving various different parts of the reproductive system. This means there are plenty of things that can potentially go wrong and make it difficult for people to have a baby together. The egg might not come out of the ovary, or the fallopian tubes might be blocked, or the sperm might not be very strong swimmers. But this doesn't have to stop a couple from having babies, thanks to a procedure called IVF (or, to give it the long name that you'll definitely forget, **IN VITRO FERTILIZATION**).

IVF means that, instead of meeting inside the body, the sperm and the egg are brought together outside the body, in a lab. Shortly afterward, the embryo is implanted into the woman's uterus to grow. Babies who started out this way used to be known as "test-tube babies," which isn't very accurate, because the baby still spends nine months growing inside a uterus, like everyone else—it just has a bit of a mini-break in the outside world for a few days when it's still a bunch of cells. A brilliant thing about IVF is that it's also a way for two men to have a child (this involves someone donating them an egg) or two women to have one (this involves someone donating them some sperm).

The first baby to be born using IVF was Louise Brown—born in Manchester, England, in 1978. Since then, nearly ten million babies have been born using IVF—that's more than the number of people who live in New York City. (Not everyone who was born using IVF has to move to New York City, though.)

KAY'S KWESTIONS

WHAT CAUSES TWINS?

I'm sure you know about twins already—when two babies grow in the uterus at the same time. One in every 65 pregnancies is a twin pregnancy, and there's

always one good twin and one evil twin. (That bit might not be totally true.) Twins can either be identical or non-identical. Identical twins occur when a fertilized egg splits into two. Nobody knows quite why this happens, but as the name suggests, they will look exactly the same. This is handy for pulling pranks, like pretending to be the other twin at school to fool your teachers, or robbing a bank and getting your identical sibling sent to prison. Non-identical twins are still similar to each other, but no more similar than any other brother or sister are. They happen when the ovaries accidentally release two eggs instead of one, like when a vending machine spits out an candy bar by mistake. Twins are also more common with IVF, when two embryos are sometimes implanted into the uterus.

WHAT'S THE POINT OF MY BELLY BUTTON?

Currently, no point whatsoever. But when you were in the uterus, the only way you could get oxygen and nutrients was through your umbilical cord—and your umbilical cord was plugged into your belly button. In fact, the proper name for your belly button is your umbilicus. The moment you were born, you were suddenly able to breathe and drink through your mouth, so most of your umbilical cord was snipped off shortly after birth. The little bit that was left behind eventually shrivelled and dried up like an old scab and fell off, leaving your belly button in its place. Most people have an innie, but a few people have an outie—it just depends how the skin heals after the umbilical cord falls off. It's traditional to eat the shrivelled, dried-up bit of umbilical cord on your eighteenth birthday. Enjoy! (Don't worry—that part's not true.)

WHY ARE MEN OFTEN TALLER THAN WOMEN?

Growth spurts come at different times for all of you, but for girls it tends to be nearer the start of puberty and for boys it's toward the end. While boys are waiting for their big upward zoom, they do an ←————————
extra couple of years of growing, and that's what gives them the advantage.

TRUE OR POO?

WHEN A WOMAN IS PREGNANT, HER FEET GET BIGGER.

TRUE As if having a baby isn't expensive enough, new moms have to buy a load of bigger shoes. The hormones of pregnancy make the foot bones separate out and the foot flatten down, which means they can go up a whole shoe size!

BABIES CRY IN THE UTERUS.

TRUE Yep, you started whining before you were even born. Typical. Doctors doing ultrasounds of babies noticed that they sometimes practice crying, although you can't actually hear them doing it all the way inside there. If you've ever wondered why babies are so good at screaming the moment they're born, it's because they've been rehearsing for months!

SPERM SWIM AT TWENTY MILES PER HOUR.

POO Sperm are a lot lazier than that—in fact, in an hour they can only go twenty centimeters, which is about *this* distance:

⟶

That's fine, though. They don't have far to travel.

CHAPTER 13

LIFE AND DEATH

HAVE YOU EVER WONDERED why you've got the same nose as your cousin? Or why the family next door is so tall that they all bang their heads on the doorframes? This is because of our genes, which get passed down through families. Not jeans (though I guess they can get passed down through families too . . .) but *genes*. Genes are the code in your bodyca set of instructions that add up to who you are. The same way everything that happens in a computer game is because of its code, every part of how your body looks and works is because of your genes. The color of your eyes, the shape of your lips, the length of your arms, the freckles on your butt, the size of your ears—it's all been coded into you.

Cells are already pretty tiny, but we'll need to look a lot closer in order to see your genes. When you zoom in, you'll see that a cell has lots of different parts.

MEMBRANE — The wall around the cell that stops all its contents from spilling out like a burst shopping bag.

CYTOPLASM — The watery goop for everything inside the cell to swim around in.

MITOCHONDRIA — Don't be fooled by the exciting name—this is just the cell's boring old battery.

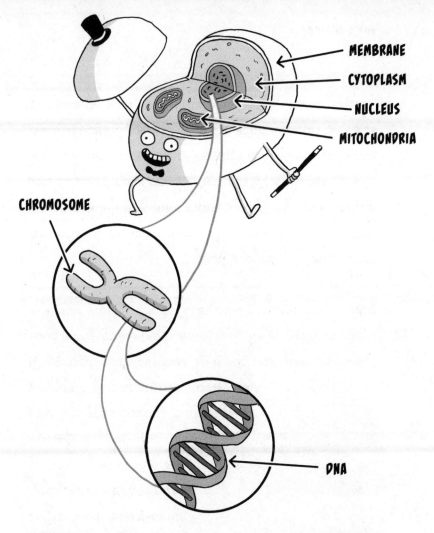

NUCLEUS — This little ball is the most important part of the cell. Inside the nucleus are forty-six chromosomes, which are arranged as twenty-three pairs (if I've done my math right). And inside these chromosomes are about twenty thousand genes, and each gene is in charge of a tiny little bit of you.

If you crank up your microscope even more, then you'll see that every gene is made up of DNA (which is short for deoxyribonucleic acid, so you'll understand why we always abbreviate it to DNA). DNA is wound around into a double spiral. I'm not quite sure why—maybe DNA just wanted to look a bit more exciting than being shaped like a brick or a potato.

Because chromosomes come in pairs, it means you have two versions of every single gene—one from your biological mom and one from your biological dad. Each gene from your mom has a kind of wrestling match with the one from your dad to decide how your body looks. Sometimes one wins, sometimes the other wins, and sometimes it's a draw—that's why you might have your mom's red hair, your dad's brown eyes, and a nose that's a mixture of them both. This is called inheritance.

The shape of DNA was discovered by the brilliant scientists Rosalind Franklin, Maurice Wilkins, James Watson, and Francis Crick. I don't know why it took four of them— I discovered how delicious an onion ring on a hot dog tastes, and there's only one of me.

334

INHERITANCE

If only one of your parents gives you the rolling-your-tongue gene (yes, it's a real thing), then you'll be able to roll your tongue. This is called a **DOMINANT GENE**.

Please don't roll your tongue in your school photos, though.

If only one of your parents gives you the long-big-toe gene (that one's real too, honest!), then you won't have a long big toe, because you need to get that gene from both of your parents. This is called a **RECESSIVE GENE**.

Remember how I told you about a condition that's much more likely to affect men? No? It was only six chapters ago—I can't believe you've forgotten that already. Honestly, I don't know why I bother. It was color blindness, and it's because it's handed down on what's called the X chromosome and it's known as an **X-LINKED GENE**. We all have X chromosomes—if you're born a girl then you have two of them, and if you're born a boy then you have one of them (and one Y chromosome). This means that if a girl has one X chromosome with the color-blindness gene, and her other X chromosome doesn't have that gene, then her vision will be unaffected. But if a boy has an X chromosome with the color-blindness gene, then he doesn't have a spare X chromosome, so he won't be able to tell his red peppers from his green peppers.

Whenever a sperm fertilizes an egg, there's around a 50 percent chance the baby's sex will be female (XX chromosomes), and around a 50 percent chance the baby's sex will be male (XY). It's basically a flip of a coin. Sometimes people are born with a mixture of male and female characteristics, which is called being intersex, something that affects around 1 percent of the population.

The person who discovered how genetics works was a monk called Gregor Mendel, who did experiments on pea plants over 150 years ago. His experiments stopped when he got a promotion at work to be in charge of his monastery, so he became too busy with admin work and organizing bell-ringing practice to fit in any more science. Who knows what else he'd have discovered if he hadn't gotten that promotion. Maybe how to project a hologram of yourself so it looks like you're at school when you're actually lying on the beach!

Some people are born with XY chromosomes, and identify as a girl, and some people are born with XX chromosomes and identify as a boy. This is known as being transgender.

Some people are born with extra chromosomes, or missing chromosomes, and this can mean that they have physical features a bit different from people who have forty-six chromosomes. You might have already heard of

However complicated a computer is—whether it's sending a rocket to Mars or playing a game where you shoot twelve-headed zombies—it only understands 0s and 1s. That's what all computer code is made from—it's just the order of the 0s and 1s that changes. Our bodies are similar. Even though we're extremely complicated, our DNA is made up of just four letters: C, G, T and A. The order they are in is unique for everyone, so it might go CGTTTAGGTACCT . . . except carrying on for billions of letters. It's like a really long Wi-Fi password. If you decided to read out your genetic code, it would take your entire lifetime. I recommend doing other things with your life, such as getting a job and going on vacation.

Down syndrome, which means there's an extra copy of chromosome number 21, and there's another condition called Turner syndrome, which affects girls and means they have one X chromosome instead of two. They can have medical problems and also learning difficulties that mean they might need a bit of extra help at school.

Some people are born with forty-six chromosomes, but there might be a faulty gene inside one of them—sort of like a spelling mistake in their DNA. What effect this has on their life depends on which gene has the error (also known as a mutation). For example, there's a genetic condition called cystic fibrosis that causes thick mucus to be produced inside the lungs and other organs, and one called sickle cell disease where the red blood cells are shaped like croissants and can get stuck in blood vessels and cause pain. There's a brand-new type of medicine called gene therapy that can help people who have a faulty gene like this. Viruses are traditionally the bad guys and not to be trusted anywhere near your body, because they love to cause havoc. But just as you're always told to see the good in people, some viruses have a positive side. In gene therapy, scientists train them to work as double agents, and sneak into cells to replace damaged genes with working ones. Clever, right?

Because this treatment hasn't been around that long, scientists are still busy doing research into it, but hopefully one day it will be able to help millions of people. You heard it here first! (Or, if you already knew about it, you heard it here second.)

CANCER

You already know that every part of your body is made up of cells, and that your body makes new cells all the time. Sometimes this process goes wrong and cells form far too fast. A lump of cells like this is known as a tumor. When we talk about how serious a tumor is, we say it's either benign or malignant. A benign tumor can cause problems by pressing on things, but the good news is it can't spread, so it should be totally curable. A malignant tumor is a tumor that can potentially spread to other parts of the body. This is more serious and is also known as cancer.

Cancer isn't actually just one illness—it's a term for hundreds of separate conditions: there are as many kinds of cancer as there are types of cells. The most common places for cancer to appear are the breasts, the lungs, the prostate, the bowel, and the skin. It mostly affects older people, but occasionally young people get cancer too.

Sometimes cancer affects more than one person in the same family. This might mean there is a mutation in one of their genes—but it doesn't mean everyone in that family will get cancer. There are some things that can make cancer more likely, such as smoking, alcohol, and spending a lot of time in the sun without wearing sunscreen. But anyone can get cancer, and it's no one's fault if they do.

Cancer is serious, but there are treatments available, and lots of people get fully cured. The type of treatment depends on a few different things, such as what part of the body has been affected, and whether or not the cancer has spread. Often patients need more than one kind of treatment.

SURGERY — Most people with cancer have some kind of operation to remove the cancerous cells. Sometimes even though a cancer is only in part of the lung or part of the breast, for example, the doctors think it's safest to remove the whole lung or the whole breast, just to be sure.

CHEMOTHERAPY — Chemotherapy (or chemo) is the name for extremely strong drugs that kill cancer cells. Chemo can be given either as tablets or as an injection into the veins. Because chemo is so powerful, it can affect perfectly healthy cells in the body too. This explains why people having this treatment can feel really tired, and why their hair sometimes falls out—but it almost always grows back after treatment is over. If someone is having chemo, then their immune system won't be working as well as yours, so it's important that you not visit them if you have a cough or a cold, in case it makes them very sick.

RADIATION THERAPY — This means firing high-energy radiation beams, a bit like X-rays, directly at the cancer. The radiation beams damage all the cells they hit, but cancer cells aren't very good at repairing themselves, so the healthy cells get better and the abnormal cells disappear.

BONE MARROW TRANSPLANT — This is a special kind of treatment for certain cancers, like lymphoma and leukemia. Lymphoma is a cancer of the lymph nodes (little glands that help you fight infection), and leukemia is a cancer of the blood. Leukemia happens when the bone marrow makes abnormal white blood cells that don't quite work as they should, and this means that people with leukemia can get infections more often. Leukemia is the most common type of cancer in children, but the good news is that it's rare and most people fully recover from it. Treatment can involve chemotherapy, radiation, and bone marrow transplants. Someone having a bone marrow transplant needs to take medicines that destroy all the cells in their bone marrow—which sounds like a strange thing to do at first, but bear with me. After that, healthy replacement cells are put into the patient's blood, and they then travel all the way to the bone marrow. This means that any new white blood cells that are made should not have cancer in them, and the leukemia is cured.

DEATH

It's very strange and very sad to know a person really well, to see them and talk to them all the time . . . and then suddenly not to have them around anymore. Unfortunately, that's just how life works: nothing can go on forever, and everything that lives will one day die— every human, every animal, every plant, every tree. Sorry to be a downer, but I'm not going to lie to you about this. Luckily, most people live a very long time—often until they are 80 or 90 or even older. The oldest person on record lived to be 122 years old! Advances in science mean that people born today are living longer than ever before. The human body is very good at fixing itself, but just like your robot butler or your best toy or favorite book (this one), it can't stay shiny and new forever.

When people get very old, wrinkles and gray hair aren't the only changes that happen to their bodies. Over time, every single organ will start to show signs of damage, and eventually those organs will stop working completely.

Sadly, some people die before they get old. Even though our bodies are marvelous, miraculous machines, sometimes they get injured so badly that they can't survive—for example, in car accidents. And sometimes people get extremely sick, and no amount of medicine can make them better.

When someone close to you dies, it can make you feel upset and stressed, like you don't know what to do with yourself or how to react. You might not want to believe that it's actually happened, and you'll have loads of questions you want to ask. At first, you might feel that life will never be the same, that you won't be able to laugh or have fun again, and that you'll always feel sad. But there is a saying that goes "time is a great healer," and it's absolutely true. It doesn't mean that you'll ever stop thinking about the person who has died, or ever stop loving them, but as the weeks and months go by you will start to feel less sad. Remember that the person you lost wouldn't want you to be sad forever; they would definitely want you to smile again. You'll always have the memories that you made together—those can never be taken away.

You won't be the only one having these feelings, and people will understand what you're going through, whether you're scared, sad, or maybe even angry. It's important that you not keep these thoughts to yourself—it might feel awkward to discuss them at first, but I promise you that you will feel better if you do.

Try not to think too much about death—what's the point? Focus instead on having as much fun as you can. Life is brilliant and precious, and we all need to make the most of it. Speaking of which, I'm off to fill a balloon with water and chuck it at my brother.

KAY'S KWESTIONS

ARE GENETIC MUTATIONS ALWAYS BAD?

I've talked about changes in genes that cause problems in the body like cancers or lung disorders, but not all genetic mutations are bad. Some people have mutations in a gene that means their muscles

I've just sent my robot butler off to the computer shop to get the key.

contract extremely effectively, and this makes them

talented at running. (I definitely don't have *that* mutation.) There are gene mutations that make people's bones stronger, so it's much harder for them to break. And there are even mutations that make it less likely you'll catch certain infections. Unfortunately, I'm unable to confirm that if you get bitten by a radioactive spider, you'll suddenly be able to climb walls, sling webs, and kiss people while hanging upside down.

IN WHICH CELLS WOULD I FIND MY GENES?

All of them! There are copies of your genetic code in every single cell in your body. You know how people always tell you to back up your data so you don't lose your homework or your photos? Well, that's exactly what the body does—trillions of times. If you unwound all the DNA in every cell of your body and laid it out in a line, it would stretch for 10 billion miles. I don't know if you've ever tried to walk for 10 billion miles, but that's one hundred times the distance from your house to the sun.

DO ANIMALS GET CANCER TOO?

I'm afraid so—cancer is a frequent cause of death throughout the animal kingdom. But there is one type of animal that never gets cancer: the naked mole rat. It's a pocket-sized rodent with big, long teeth and . . . it's very ugly. I'm not normally the sort of person to judge someone by their looks, but boy oh boy, this thing looks bad. Maybe nature thought the naked mole rat had enough problems, being so butt-ugly, and spared it from getting cancer. Whatever the reason, scientists are busy looking at this little gremlin's genes to see if it can help us find a cure for cancer in humans.

TRUE OR POO?

SCIENTISTS HAVE SENT BACKUPS OF HUMAN DNA INTO SPACE, IN CASE THE EARTH IS WIPED OUT.

TRUE A cheery thought, but scientists decided to come up with a plan B, and sent the genetic code of a bunch of humans into space on a computer. Look up—it's currently whizzing around 250 miles above your head in the International Space Station. People they chose include Stephen Hawking (a brilliant scientist), Stephen Colbert (a talk-show host—maybe they're important in space?), and a few other famous people not named Stephen. I can't believe they didn't use my DNA—very disappointing.

IT'S NOT YOUR FAULT THAT YOU DON'T LIKE CABBAGE.

TRUE Well, it might not be. Certain people have a gene that makes some vegetables taste so bitter that they're too disgusting to eat—particularly things like broccoli, cabbage, and cauliflower. Unfortunately, screaming, "I can't eat it! It's genetic!" is unlikely to get you out of eating your veggies.

ALL HUMANS ARE 99 PERCENT IDENTICAL.

TRUE Whatever the color of your skin or your hair, whether you've got the tiniest button nose or one that touches your phone screen when you're typing, whether you're the height of your desk or the height of the ceiling, your DNA is almost identical. If you find any person on the planet and look at their genetic code, less than one percent of it will be different from yours. Even your math teacher's. (Sorry about that.)

CHAPTER 14
GERMS

GERMS ARE EVERYWHERE. Literally trillions of them, all over the place. There's no point looking up hazmat suits on eBay, because germs are impossible to avoid. Don't panic, though—the world couldn't actually survive without them. We need germs inside our gut to help us digest food. Most other species of animals would go extinct without germs, and almost all plants would die out, because they need bacteria to produce their fuel. Worst of all, we wouldn't be able to make cheese, so dinner would be ruined.

But not all germs are our friends. Sometimes bugs that shouldn't be inside our bodies can launch an invasion and cause coughs and colds, puking, and pooping. (Those guys just love making a mess.) Let's meet some of them—the good, the bad, and the pukey.

BACTERIA

Bacteria are only one cell big, but they pack a punch and can cause all sorts of illnesses to make you miserable. Ear infections, throat infections, skin infections—you name it, they can infect it. They're also experts at causing food poisoning, as well as some very serious conditions like meningitis. They come in all sorts of different shapes, from blobs to snakes to spirals.

CARTOONIFICATION DEVICE

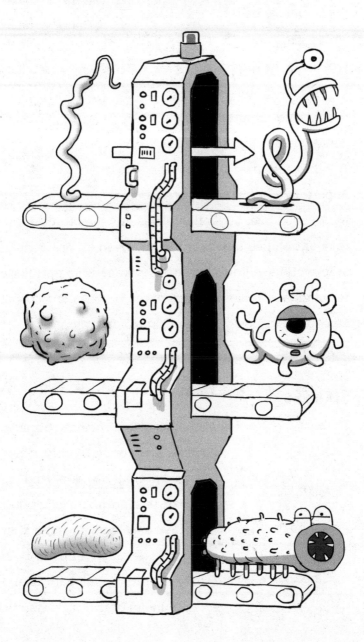

But for every villain there's always a superhero, and we have antibiotics to fight any bacteria that have sneaked in somewhere they shouldn't.

Alexander Fleming discovered **penicillin**, the very first antibiotic, when he accidentally let some mold grow in his lab. He won the Nobel Prize for this discovery—the biggest prize in all of science. When I accidentally let mold grow in my bedroom, I just get told off by my husband.

Antibiotics are one of the most important medical discoveries of all time—in fact, they have saved over 100 million lives. It's important not to take antibiotics unless you really need to, or they can stop working altogether—this is known as antibiotic resistance. It's like the story of the boy who cried wolf (except "the boy who cried antibiotic" sounds a lot more boring).

VIRUSES

Put some stronger glasses on now, because viruses are about twenty times smaller than bacteria. And I'm not talking about computer viruses like the one that made my robot butler smash up my bathroom, I mean horrid little germs.

You're only half human. No, you're not half goat (although that would explain the smell). About 50 percent of the cells in your body are actually helpful bacteria who've set up home there. Maybe you should charge them rent?

They work by squeezing into healthy cells and taking control of them. It's like if someone moved into your spare room, then kicked you out of your own house.

When these virus-filled cells spread, they can make you ill. Viruses you might have heard of include the common cold, flu, coronavirus, and that itchy blister factory known as chicken pox.

FUNGI

You've eaten a lot of fungus before, and I'm not just talking about mushrooms (yuck)—they're also in salami, cheese, soy sauce—you can't escape them. Fungi of any type prefer to live where it's dark and damp, like on the forest floor, at the bottom of your trash can, and . . . on your feet, lurking inside your socks and shoes.

FUN TIE

FUNGUS TIE

A fungal infection between your toes is called athlete's foot. You don't have to be an athlete to get it, so I'm afraid you can't stay safe just by avoiding PE. Luckily, there are antifungal creams to treat it, so you can wave goodbye to your foot fungus just as quickly as I throw away those mushrooms on my plate.

PROTOZOA

Protozoa is the name given to a whole load of different germs, like a (highly infectious) pick 'n' mix. They all have a couple of things in common: they're one cell big, and you don't want any of them taking a staycation inside your body.

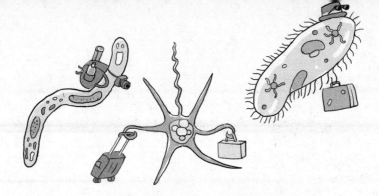

Diseases they cause include nasties like malaria (which causes bad fevers) and dysentery (which causes really bad diarrhea).

KEEPING YOURSELF HEALTHY

Because they're so small, germs usually get inside our bodies without us realizing (unless a friend sneezes in your face, in which case maybe you need to find some replacement friends?). Even though your body has all sorts of ways of defending itself against germs, it's much better to stop them from getting in there in the first place.

WASH YOUR HANDS

Your hands are—how can I say this without offending you?—utterly grotesque. They're constantly

Three in ten people don't use soap when they wash their hands after going to the bathroom . . . and one in ten people doesn't wash up at all. There's a medical term for people like that: absolutely disgusting.

throwing a hideous party where all the guests are bacteria and viruses. You already know (I hope) how important it is to wash your hands after going to the bathroom, but it's not just poop that germs love—they'll hang out anywhere: toys, light switches, door handles, you name it. You should always wash your hands before touching food, but it's good to get into the habit of washing them much more often than that. And when I say wash your hands, I don't mean a pathetic wiggling of your fingers under a barely dribbling tap—you're effectively waving germs straight through to the VIP area if you do that. I mean properly, with soap and water.

HOW TO WASH YOUR HANDS

You should spend a minimum of twenty seconds washing your hands, which is how long it takes to sing "Happy Birthday" twice, or chant "ADAM KAY IS EXCELLENT—HE SHOULD BE THE KING" ten times. I generally go for the second option.

When you cough, do it into your elbow, and when you sneeze, do it into a tissue and throw it away immediately. Try not to sneeze into your hands—they're gross enough as it is—but if you do, wash them right away. If your grandpa has a handkerchief that he keeps in his pocket, you can tell him he's got an absolute zoo of bacteria in there, and if he ever thinks about licking it and wiping your face . . . run!

IMMUNE SYSTEM

Even though your body has loads of different ways of protecting you from intruders (those little hairs up your nose, for example, and the mucus in your trachea), you can't guard every wall of the castle, and some germs will inevitably find their way in. Thankfully, your immune system—your built-in antivirus software—is always on duty inside, ready to evict any unwelcome visitors. Eating well, staying active, and getting plenty of rest will make your immune system strong enough to kick the bacterial butts of any germs stupid enough to come your way. (Yeah, I know—I go on about this a lot. I'm not even being bribed to say it by broccoli farmers and bed manufacturers.) The stars of your immune system are your white blood cells, which you might remember from back when we chatted about blood *all* those pages ago. White blood cells are green-colored cells that . . . Hold on, I might need to read that chapter again. Oh yeah, that's right. White blood cells are white-colored cells that seek out anything that shouldn't be there and fight it off. Fight! Fight! Fight!

The white blood cell's secret weapons are called **ANTIBODIES**. When a white blood cell spots an enemy invader, it designs these special antibody bullets, then fires out loads and loads of them.

When an enemy cell has been destroyed, a different type of white cell called a **MACROPHAGE** comes along and eats it. (Macrophage actually means "massive eater.") Savage

but delicious. The first time your body meets a new kind of germ, it takes a while to design special antibodies to attack it, but the next time that germ comes along, those antibodies are all lined up and ready to fire. This is called immunity—if you're immune to a bug, then you have antibodies to combat it and it can't harm you. It's like having a photo of a dangerous criminal, and as soon as they turn up . . . *Zap! Chomp!* Eaten whole. These guys don't mess around.

LYMPHATIC SYSTEM

Along with your blood vessels, your body has a secret second network of tubes and tunnels that's just used by your white blood cells—a bit like the way some big buildings have elevators that are just for fire-fighters, in case there's an emergency. It's called your lymphatic system, and it carries white blood cells around in a fluid called lymph. Strange word, that: lymph. Sounds like I've just made it up. (I haven't, honest.) Your lymphatic system also has lots of little lumps of tissue called **LYMPH NODES**. If you've ever had a throat infection and you've felt those painful little lumps in your neck, those are your lymph nodes getting bigger as they fill up with white blood cells to help you fight the infection.

Other parts of your lymphatic system include your tonsils and a little organ that lives near your stomach called the **SPLEEN**, which again sounds totally made up. I reckon the naming committee got to 5 p.m. on a Friday and Clive just said, "You know what? It's been a long week—spleen and lymph will do."

VACCINES

Good news—there's a shortcut to getting antibodies against a bug without ever being infected. Please welcome to the stage . . . vaccines. A vaccine is a tiny dose of a dead or very weak germ. You usually get it through an injection, and your body develops antibodies, so the real version of the bug will never bother you. I'm not going to pretend that the shots don't hurt at all, but they're really not that bad—and it's about five million times better than catching the diseases they save you from. Oh, and you've already had most of the vaccines you'll ever need back when you were tiny, so stop moaning.

Some people, for some reason, think that vaccines are dangerous for you, or they contain chemicals that can cause damage, or even lead to conditions such as autism, but that is absolute ********. Sorry, my editor deleted that word for being too rude. It's absolute ********.

Hmm, she deleted it again. Okay, fine—it's absolute nonsense. Vaccines are totally safe, and they save millions of lives every year.

ALLERGIES

We all overreact sometimes. Maybe you drop your ice cream and have a massive tantrum about it. Or your friend forgets your birthday, so you break into his house in the middle of the night and fill all his curtain rods with shrimp so his house stinks like a seafood restaurant. (Maybe that was just me.) Anyway, your immune system can overreact too, and that's exactly what allergies are: your body treating perfectly normal things like enemies.

You can have allergies to lots of things, such as pollen or grass (this is called hay fever), certain types of food, or even cat and dog hair. (I'm sorry, Pippin, there are some people you're not allowed to slobber on.)

Allergies make your body send out unnecessary antibodies, and this gives you symptoms like wheezes or sneezes or itchy eyes or skin rashes. Normally, allergies aren't too bad, and you just have to try your best to avoid the things that cause the symptoms. Some people's allergies are a bit more serious and they have to take medicines called antihistamines to help the symptoms calm down. The good news is that lots of people grow out of allergies as they get older.

Some people's allergies are *extremely* serious, and mean that their throat swells up when they're exposed to certain things and they can even stop breathing. This is called **ANAPHYLAXIS**. You might know someone who is extremely allergic to something like bee stings or peanuts or latex (a type of rubber), and you'll already know how serious it can be. If someone has a severe peanut allergy, then no one else in that room should eat peanuts. People who are at risk of anaphylaxis should always carry a special kind of injection around with them called an EpiPen, which can be used in an emergency to inject epinephrine into their leg and save their life.

INFECTIOUS DISEASES

FOOD POISONING

Have you ever eaten something and then felt ill? Not "Ugh, I think I ate a bit too much chocolate" kind of ill, but "running at full speed to the bathroom before liquid shoots out of both ends" kind of ill? This means there were bacteria in your beefburger or viruses in your vindaloo, and we call it food poisoning. It might have happened because the person who prepared the food didn't wash their hands (see, told you it was important) or it had been left out of the fridge for too long or not cooked well enough. Food poisoning is no fun at all, but the buttsquirts usually get better after a day or two. (I've applied to join the naming committee, so hopefully "buttsquirts" will be an official medical term before long.)

CORONAVIRUS

You probably already know about coronavirus, because of the pandemic (a scientific term for an infection that has spread across the whole world) that began in early 2020. Because it was a brand-new virus, there were no vaccines to stop people from catching it and no special treatment for the people who did.

Coronavirus is very contagious and is spread by an infectious person coughing or even just speaking or breathing. It can also be passed on by someone putting their hand on an infected surface, then touching their eyes, nose, or mouth. Eventually, people all over the world had to stay in their homes to stop it from spreading, because otherwise hospitals wouldn't have been able to cope, since they only have a certain amount of beds, staff, and equipment. The virus caused a disease called **COVID-19**. It stands for COronaVIrus Disease 2019, because it was first discovered in 2019. So I guess if I ever caused a disease, it would be known as ADKAD-80 (ADam KAy Disease 1980).

Most people who caught it had very mild symptoms or even no symptoms at all, but some people developed extremely serious medical conditions, especially in their lungs. Many people died as a result, particularly those who were older or who already had other illnesses. It's likely that other brand-new infections will appear in the years to come, but hopefully countries will learn from this pandemic how to stop new viruses causing so much harm.

THE COMMON COLD

Do you really need me to tell you what a cold is? Fine. It's a virus that affects your nose. The younger you are, the more colds you get, because you haven't made as many antibodies as you have when you're older. You probably get about five colds a year. That's a whole lot of snot. The cold virus is constantly changing, which is why you keep catching it: you developed immunity to the one you had last time, but not the one that's going around now. This is also why there's no vaccine for it— by the time we came up with one, the virus would have changed shape and the vaccine would be useless. Sorry, the snot's here to stay.

MENINGITIS

Meningitis means germs have infected the covering of the brain. Although it isn't common, it can be extremely serious. Meningitis causes a headache, a rash, and a stiff neck, and it makes people very sensitive to bright lights. Meningitis that's caused by bacteria is a medical emergency and needs to be treated with strong antibiotics right away. Meningitis caused by a virus is generally less serious and often gets better with rest. There's now a vaccination for the most serious kinds of meningitis, and it saves the lives of thousands of young people every year. Hooray for vaccines!

VERRUCAS

Verrucas are strange little warts that crop up on the bottom of your feet. They're caused by viruses and often have tiny black dots in the middle of them. They're very contagious (so don't pick them!) and they love it when it's damp, so that's why you have to be extra careful in swimming pools and locker rooms. Water shoes aren't just a fashion statement.

KAY'S QUESTIONS

WHAT IS BELLY BUTTON FLUFF?

Finally, someone's asking the important questions in life. Belly button fluff is made up of bits of cotton from your T-shirt, dust, dead skin, and, of course, loads of

Woohoo! It's fixed! I can type the letter Q as much as I like. The queen quickly cooked a quince and quail quiche. It's a shame we're practically at the end of the boo . I mean the boo . Uh-oh.

bacteria. No two people have the same types of bacteria in their belly buttons, so the police could use belly button bacteria instead of fingerprints to identify people. (Although I think fingerprints are probably more convenient and a bit less gross.)

WHY DO I NEED SHOTS WHEN I TRAVEL ABROAD?

If you're lucky enough to be heading off on a vacation far away, you might be told you need to have some shots before you're allowed to go. These are vaccinations, a bit like the ones you have growing up, except they are for germs that don't live where you do but are common in the place you're visiting. They include such delights as rabies, typhoid, and yellow fever. Normally, getting shots means you get a bit of sympathy from your friends, but you don't when you're having travel shots, because it means you're about to go on an amazing vacation and they aren't.

IS THE FIVE-SECOND RULE SAFE?

Your family might use the five-second rule—if a piece of food falls on the ground but it's there for less than five seconds, then it's fine to pick it up and eat it. Maybe they think that bacteria take a slow, leisurely walk over to that fry you dropped? Or maybe they don't want to give you one of *their* fries as a replacement? The truth is that the millisecond the food hits the floor, it is instantly covered with incredible numbers of bacteria. Do you really want to risk spending your entire weekend sitting on the toilet just because you decided to rescue a fallen fry?

TRUE OR POO?

WASHING YOUR HANDS WITH HOT WATER KILLS MORE BACTERIA THAN COLD WATER.

POO   I was surprised by this when I first learned it too. The cold water is just as effective when washing your hands as the hot water—the important things are using soap and washing for long enough. I mean, you could kill bacteria by using extremely hot water, but it would have to be so hot that all your skin would blister off agonizingly. You're probably better off using soap, to be honest.

SOME BACTERIA GLOW IN THE DARK.

TRUE   Bioluminescent bacteria (to give them their proper name) are microscopic light bulbs that live underwater. It seems a bit unfair that we humans have bacteria that make us puke, but if you're an octopus, your bacteria give you an all-night disco.

YOUR PHONE HAS POOP ON IT.

TRUE   Hahahaha. Yep, if you've got a phone, then you've probably got a poo-covered screen. If you want to avoid this, then the best way is not to take your phone into the bathroom with you—and there's the added advantage that you can't accidentally drop it into the toilet.

CONCLUSION

RIGHT, THERE YOU GO. I've now officially taught you everything there is to know about the body. Every single last bit. Nothing missed whatsoever.

Oh, hang on. Actually, I forgot something:

THERE'S a condition called exploding-head syndrome. It sounds a little dramatic (to say the least), but it's actually nothing to worry about. It happens to lots of people when they're lying in bed—the second they're about to fall asleep, they suddenly hear an enormous *BANG!* Luckily, it doesn't mean there's anything serious going on, and even better, your brain hasn't exploded into a trillion pieces, so no one needs to repaint your bedroom.

There. All done—that's all you need to know. Finished. Promise.

Nope. I was wrong. One last thing, then we're definitely 100 percent done:

> You blink for a month every year. That's an entire *month* when you should be awake but your brain has decided to press the pause button. Just think what you could achieve in a month if you didn't blink—you could bake seven hundred cakes, or learn another language, or teach your robot butler how to play tennis. Although if you didn't blink then your eyes would get really sore, so it's probably best that you do, actually.

Phew. All over. That's it. You can stop reading now.

No, sorry. Not quite. I just realized I missed something else:

WHEN you sit in a classroom, you're breathing in your friends' (and your teacher's) farts. And not just a tiny bit either. Every week you breathe in enough pure, undiluted fart to fill up a big bottle of lemonade. Maybe open the window in there?

Done. Finally.

Any questions? (If you've got any questions, go back to the start and read the whole book again.)

MEDICAL CERTIFICATE
This is to certify that

- - - - - - - - - - - - - - - - - - - -

*(Write your name here—really neatly, though.
This is going up in your office.)*

has learned all about butts and blood and lungs
and mucus and nose hair and elbows and pee and
leeches and brains and skin and toenails and
bacteria and hamstrings and poop and livers and
earwax and robot butlers and teeth and snot and
bones and those little insects that live in your
eyelashes and kidneys and a bit more poop . . .

And is now a fully qualified doctor.*

- - - - - - - - - - - - - - - - - - - -

*(Write the date here. Neater than you did before —
that looked awful.)*

**

Adam Kay
Doctor, writer, and incredible genius

* Pretty much.
** Please don't use my signature to steal all my money.
Or, if you do, make sure you buy something nice.

A NOTE FOR THE PRINTERS:

Please put this next bit in a really, really small font so that everyone thinks I did the entire book on my own, without any help at all. Lots of love, Adam

ACKNOWLEDGMENTS

To James, my hero/husband.

To Cath Summerhayes and Jessica Cooper, my amazing agents.

To Henry Paker, my ingenious illustrator.

To Ruth Knowles and Holly Harris, my extraordinary editors.

To Alison Romig and Beverly Horowitz, my awesome American publishers.

To Francesca Dow and Tom Weldon, my phenomenal publishers.

To my favorite (and only) nephews and niece: Noah, Zareen, Lenny, Sidney, and Jesse.

To all my lecturers at medical school—I'm really sorry if I remembered everything wrong and have passed on colossal amounts of misinformation to thousands of young readers.

To Jan Bielecki and Wendy Shakespeare for turning a rambling, misspelled Word document full of typos into an actual beautiful book.

To every single Puffin and Penguin listed at the back of the book. You all deserve an extra bucket of fish.

To Pippin, even though she tried to sabotage this book at every turn.

To Justin Myers, the sorcerer of sentences.

To Mo Khan, medical maestro.

To Hannah Farrell, knowledge ninja.

And, finally, to YOU! My brilliant readers. Oh, sorry, not you— I was talking to the person behind you.

APPENDIX

Still does nothing.

GLOSSARY

Doctors learn fifteen thousand new words about the body and the different ways it goes wrong—that's more words than you need to be fluent in a whole language! I didn't include all fifteen thousand in this section; otherwise the book would have been too heavy for you to lift.

ALVEOLI *(al-VEE-oh-lee)* Millions of little bags in your lungs. Great for oxygen transfer, not so great for carrying your shopping.

AMYGDALA *(a-MIG-dah-lah)* A part of your brain that you use for feeling things. I don't mean feeling things like being tickled by a malfunctioning robot butler, I mean feeling emotions.

ANOSMIA *(an-OZ-mee-ah)* Not being able to smell things. Very handy if you live with Pippin.

ANTIBIOTICS *(AN-tie-bye-AH-tiks)* Medicines that fight bacteria. I'm not totally sure, but I think they use tiny laser guns.

AORTA *(ay-OR-tah)* Your body's main artery. (No offense, radial artery.) It carries blood full of oxygen out of the heart and off around the body.

ATRIA *(AY-tree-uh)* The sections at the top of your heart where the blood flows in. It also means the foyer of a building—architects need to come up with their own words. Maybe Clive will sue them.

BORBORYGMUS *(BOR-bor-IG-mus)* The gurgles and grumbles and rumbles that your intestines make if you haven't eaten enough cake recently.

BRONCHI *(BRON-kye)* The main bronchial tubes that go from your windpipe into your lungs. Good to have if you're a fan of breathing.

BRONCHIOLES *(BRON-key-ohls)* Smaller tubes that branch off your bronchi. The bronchi and bronchioles are such good friends that they even hang out next to each other in the glossary.

BUTT *(BUTT)* This isn't a proper medical word. Why's it in this section?

CANCELLOUS *(can-SELL-us)* **BONE** One of the layers in your bones—it's got lots of holes in it, but don't worry, it's supposed to.

CEMENTUM *(se-MENT-um)* Tissue that glues your teeth into your jaw. Basically cement. (But with an "um" at the end.)

CEREBELLUM *(ser-uh-BELL-um)* A small part of your brain that's in charge of balance, so it's very important for tightrope walkers. It means "little brain"—cute!

CEREBRUM *(ser-EE-brum)* The main part of your brain. Does a few minor things like thinking, moving your body around, and keeping you alive. No biggie.

CERUMEN *(ser-OO-men)* A fancy word for earwax, in case you ever need to say earwax at a chic party. (This won't happen much.)

CERVIX *(SER-viks)* A doughnut-shaped structure between the uterus and the vagina. Cervix is Latin for "neck," which is slightly confusing because it's nowhere near the neck.

CHROMOSOME *(KRO-moh-sohm)* A structure that lives in your cells and contains your genes. Not to be confused with your closet, which lives in your bedroom and contains your jeans.

COCCYX *(KOK-siks)* The lowest part of your spine, also known as your tailbone. It's the shortest word with three Cs in it.

COCHLEA *(KOK-lee-ah)* The part of your inner ear that converts sounds into messages for nerves to send to your brain. Cochlea is ancient Greek for "snail," because it's snail-shaped (not because it sends the messages really slowly).

DEMODEX *(DEM-uh-deks)* Mighty mites that might live in your eyelashes.

DEXTROCARDIA *(DECKS-troh-KAR-dee-ah)* A rare condition where the heart is on the right side of the body. (It's normally on the left, if you didn't read the book that carefully.)

DIAPHRAGM *(DIE-ah-fram)* The big dome-shaped muscle that makes you breathe and separates your lungs from your lunch.

EMBRYO *(EM-bree-oh)* A ball of cells that can do a pretty clever magic trick: turning into a baby. (Embryos can't do the magic trick of pulling a rabbit out of a hat—they haven't developed hands yet.)

ENZYME *(EN-zime)* A chemical that breaks up food so your body can use it. Most enzymes have names that end in *-ase*. For example, lipase is an enzyme that breaks up fat, amylase is an enzyme that breaks up carbohydrates, and a suitcase is what you take on vacation.

EPIGLOTTIS *(EP-ee-GLOT-iss)* A flap in the throat that stops your Cheerios from going into your windpipe.

ESOPHAGUS *(uh-SOF-uh-gus)* How does food get from your throat to your stomach? A catapult, maybe? Teleportation? Or down the esophagus? (Clue: it's the esophagus.)

ESTROGEN *(EES-tra-jen)* The main female hormone, which is in charge of the changes that happen during puberty.

FECES *(FEE-sees)* A fancy word for poop.

FIBRIN *(FIE-brin)* Fibrin makes scabs, and scabs stop you from bleeding to death. Good old fibrin.

FLATUS *(FLAY-tus)* The expulsion of intestinal gas. Okay, fine—farting.

GLOSSARY *(GLO-suh-ree)* The boring pages at the back of a book where there's a big list of explanations about what different words mean.

GLUTEUS MAXIMUS *(GLOO-tee-us MAX-im-us)* If you didn't have your gluteus maximus muscles, then you wouldn't be able to move your hips. Also you wouldn't have a butt, because it's your butt.

HEMOGLOBIN *(HEE-moh-GLOW-bin)* Do you like that your blood carries oxygen? That's all because of hemoglobin. Do you like how your blood is red? Hemoglobin again. Do you like how delicious pizza is? Nothing to do with hemoglobin.

HETEROCHROMIA *(HET-er-oh-KROH-mee-ah)* If one eye is a different color from the other, then you've got heterochromia. Or one of your colored contact lenses has fallen out.

HIPPOCAMPUS *(HIP-oh-KAM-puss)* A part of your brain that helps you remember. Remember?

HORMONES *(HOR-mones)* The body's messaging system. The name comes from a Greek word meaning "to cheer on." Woo! Go, hormones!

HYPOTHALAMUS *(HY-poh-THAL-ah-mus)* A bit of your brain that tells you if you're hungry or sleepy. Pippin's hypothalamus must be massive.

INTERCOSTAL *(IN-ter-KOS-tal)* **MUSCLES** Little muscles between your ribs that make your lungs move. They're so bossy.

JOINT *(JOYNT)* Where a bone joins to another bone it's called a joint. If your joints are sore, maybe you need some jointment.

KERATIN *(CARE-ah-tin)* The material that makes your hair so delicious. Sorry, not delicious, strong. Stop eating your hair.

LOBE *(LOWB)* Organs like your brain, your lungs, your liver, and your kidneys are divided into sections called lobes. Your ear also has lobes—I think it got jealous.

LOBULE *(LOB-yool)* A lobule is a tiny lobe. This doesn't mean that a granule is a tiny gran.

MACROPHAGE *(MAK-roh-faje)* I'm a person who likes eating pizza, Pippin is a dog who likes eating fox poop, and a macrophage is a white blood cell who likes eating germs.

METACARPALS *(met-ah-KAR-puhls)* The five bones in the palm of each hand. If you've got more than five of them then please see a doctor because something's gone wrong.

METATARSALS *(met-ah-TAR-suhls)* The five long bones in each foot. A bit like the metacarpals in your hand, but stinkier.

NEPHRONS *(NEF-rons)* I don't know why the kidney cells have got a name so similar to "neurons." Probably just to make it extra complicated for you to remember which is which.

NEURONS *(NEW-rons)* You might call them your brain cells and nerve cells but "neuron" is the official name they have on their passports.

OCCIPITAL *(ok-SIP-ih-tal)* **LOBES** Enjoying reading this glossary? No? Oh, how rude. When your eyes read a word on this page, they send it to the occipital lobes of your brain.

ONYCHOPHAGIA *(on-ee-koh-FAY-jia)* Biting your nails. There are medical names for all sorts of horrible behavior. Mucophagia means eating snot, coprophagia means eating poop, and most disgusting of all—fungophagia means eating mushrooms.

PARIETAL *(par-EYE-ah-tal)* **LOBES** The part of your brain that feels touch and pain. Oh, that rhymes—hopefully they'll put this book in the poetry section now.

PERIOSTEUM *(per-ee-OS-te-um)* The outer layer of a bone. If it's got spicy sauce on it, then it's called peri-peri-osteum.

PINNA *(PIN-ah)* The flappy bit of your ear.

PIPPIN *(PIP-in)* My dog. She's lovely or awful, depending on whether she's just jumped into a muddy swamp.

PLACENTA *(plah-SENT-ah)* An organ that develops in the uterus during pregnancy and delivers food to the growing baby. Like a constant take-out service (where the only food is blood).

POOP *(POOP)* That's not a medical word either! Get it out of my nice, sensible glossary!

RADIAL *(RAY-dee-ul)* **ARTERY** An artery at the bottom of the arm where you can feel your pulse. Mine is still furious with me after I said the aorta was the body's main artery earlier.

RECTUM *(REC-tum)* The last stop on a poop's journey before it plops into the toilet. (Or onto the carpet, if you're Pippin yesterday—that was not funny.)

ROBOT BUTLER *(RO-bot BUT-ler)* Haven't you bought one yet?

SALIVA *(sal-EYE-vah)* Spit, slobber, dribble, drool. Keeps your mouth moist and helps you swallow.

SEPTUM *(SEP-tum)* A piece of cartilage in your nose that means you have two nostrils rather than one big snot-hole.

SYNOVIAL *(sy-NO-vee-al)* **FLUID** The liquid inside your joints. Without synovial fluid, it would sound like your knees were full of potato chips every time you walked. *Crunch, crunch, crunch.*

TESTOSTERONE *(tes-TOS-ter-own)* The main male hormone, responsible for the changes in puberty.

TRACHEA *(tra-KEY-ah)* The windpipe, which connects your mouth to your lungs. Not to be confused with the bagpipes, which make a horrendous noise.

TUMOR *(TEW-mer)* A lump that forms when cells grow too fast. Tumors can be cancerous (malignant) or not cancerous (benign).

UMBILICAL *(um-BILL-uh-cal)* **CORD** The tube that runs from the placenta to a baby's belly button. It gets cut off when you're born—luckily the umbilical cord doesn't have any nerves in it, so this doesn't hurt. Although babies are always screaming anyway, so you wouldn't know.

URETERS *(YUR-eh-ters)* More tubes. These ones carry pee from the kidneys to the bladder—what a terrible job they've got.

URETHRA *(yur-EETH-ra)* What is this, the tube section? The urethra is a tube that carries the pee from the bladder to the outside world. Splosh!

UTERUS *(YEW-ter-us)* The part of the female reproductive system where a baby can grow.

UVULA *(YEW-vya-la)* The dangly bit that hangs down at the back of your throat, like a fleshy wind chime.

VENA CAVA *(VEE-na KAY-vah)* The biggest vein in your body—it's wide enough to fit a quarter inside. (Please don't try this.)

VENTRICLE *(VEN-tri-cul)* The sections at the bottom of your heart where the blood pumps out. Ventricle is the Latin word for "stomach"—those Romans had their anatomy pretty confused. It's a shame I didn't write this book in time for them to read it.

ZEBRA *(ZEE-bra)* A big animal—looks like someone's painted a horse. Nothing to do with anatomy, but I thought I should probably end on a Z word.

INDEX

FURTHER INFORMATION

You might want to know a bit more about things you've read in the book, and no offense, but there's zero chance I'm giving you my phone number. Instead, here are some resources you might find helpful.

KIDS' HEALTH

If you're worried about anything that's going on with your body, then you should speak to a grown-up about it, and they might take you to a doctor or a nurse or a pharmacist or a bakery (if they need to pick up some bread first). But if you're interested in knowing more about anything from allergies to zinc deficiency, then this website is an excellent place to start.

KIDSHEALTH.ORG

EMERGENCIES

Sometimes you might need to get urgent medical help for you or someone else. In an emergency you should call 911 and they will send an ambulance. Emergencies mean things like a serious accident, or if someone has collapsed or stopped breathing, or if they are having a seizure, experiencing bad chest pain, or they suddenly can't speak or move an arm or leg.

It's important that you only call 911 for real emergencies.

FIRST AID

First aid means knowing what to do in an emergency before medical help arrives. This website teaches you lots of useful skills; for example, how to help someone who has broken a bone or is having an asthma attack. The lessons are written by the Red Cross, who are first aid experts. Not to be confused with red sauce, which is another name for ketchup.

REDCROSS.ORG

CHANGE4LIFE

If you want to know more about healthy eating and exercise, then UK based Change4Life is full of sweaty recipes and delicious workouts to keep your body in tip-top condition. Sorry, I meant delicious recipes and sweaty workouts.

CHANGE4LIFE.CO.UK

ORGAN DONATION

If you want to know more about organ donation, then you can read about it here. Important: please do not send them one of your kidneys—that's not how it works.

ORGANDONOR.GOV

ASTHMA KIDS

This website has loads of information on living with asthma as well as exercises for you to do. (I mean quizzes—they won't make you run a half-marathon.) The website is based in Australia, so I recommend you don't call them unless you've saved up a lot of pocket money for the phone bill.

ASTHMAKIDS.ORG.AU

EPILEPSY

If you or someone you know is diagnosed with epilepsy then you might have a lot of questions, and this website should be able to answer them!

EPILEPSY.COM

ERIC

If you have problems with your pee or poop, then ERIC is there to help. (ERIC is a brilliant charity, by the way; it's not just a guy named Eric.)

ERIC.ORG.UK

YOUR LIFE YOUR VOICE

If you're under the age of nineteen and are worried about anything at all, then Your Life Your Voice is there for you. It's free and confidential, which means no one will find out that you've chatted to them or anything you've talked about. As well as a helpline and an online chat service, they also have lots of useful information on everything from stress to smoking, and message boards where you can get support from other young people in similar situations.

YOURLIFEYOURVOICE.ORG

CHILD MIND INSTITUTE

The Child Mind Institute is an independent nonprofit that provides help, support, and information on mental health. Whatever difficulties you're having—whether it's anxiety, ADHD, anger, or anorexia—they are there to help. (They don't just deal with conditions starting with the letter A, by the way.)

CHILDMIND.ORG

AUTISM SOCIETY

If you want to know more about autism, or how to support your friends or siblings who are autistic, then this site is full of great information.

AUTISM-SOCIETY.ORG

ASPCA

The American Society for the Prevention of Cruelty to Animals® (ASPCA®) is a wonderful charity that finds happy new homes for animals who have been abandoned or mistreated. Their website also has lots of information about how to look after your pet. Pippin will be extremely pleased I've mentioned them.

ASPCA.ORG

CREDITS

MANAGEMENT
Francesca Dow
Barbara Marcus
Tom Weldon

EDITORIAL
Holly Harris
Beverly Horowitz
James Kay
Ruth Knowles
Alison Romig
Wendy Shakespeare

DESIGN
Sylvia Bi
Jan Bielecki
Anna Billson
Cathy Bobak
Jacqui McDonough
Dan Newman

COPYEDITORS
Kimberley Davis
Colleen Fellingham

PROOFREADERS
Petra Bryce
Marcus Fletcher
Jane Tait

INDEXER
Ruth Ellis

READERS & CONSULTANTS
Dr. Eleanor Draeger
Dr. Mo Khan
Jo Lincoln
Justin Myers
Rosie Sykes
Felicity Trotman
Dr. George Tse
Dr. Matthew Tse
Dr. Hannah Walch

EBOOK
Odile de Caires
Jessica Dunn
Thomas Marquet
Bea Pantoja

AUDIO
Shannon Ellis
Amber Kassianou-Hannan
Ashleigh James
James Keyte
Tallulah Lyons
Laura Marlow
Chloe Rose
Helena Sheffield

PRODUCTION
Michael Martin
Erica Pascal
Jamie Taylor
Tim Terhune

INVENTORY
Katherine Whelan
Megan Williams

FINANCE
Aimee Buchanan
Jamie Clark
Duc Luong
James Perry
Rich Romano

CONTRACTS
Mary Fox
Kiran Halaith
Amy Meyer

RIGHTS
Maeve Banham
Anne Bowman
Susanne Evans
Beth Fennell
Lena Petzke

MARKETING & COMMUNICATIONS
John Adamo
Simon Armstrong
Hannah Bourne
Rosamund Hutchison
Kate Keating
Caroline Maddison
Kelly McGauly
Dusty Miller
Michelle Nathan
Jannine Saunders
Adrienne Waintraub

PARTNERSHIPS
Alesha Bonser
Nina Harrison

SALES
Kat Baker
Hannah Best
Toni Budden
Karin Burnik
Enid Chaban
Felicia Frazier
Michael Gentile
Becky Green
Han Ismail
Sophie Marston
Geraldine McBride
Sarah Roscoe
Mark Santella
Rozzie Todd
Becki Wells

BIBLIOGRAPHIC METADATA
Leah Boulton
Jack Lowe

OPERATIONS
Melissa Donaldson
Sally Rideout
Tamar Schwartz

PRINTERS
Amelia Douglas
Jodi Foulger